THE Culinary CANINE

Great Chefs Cook for Their Dogs—And So Can You!

Written by Kathryn Levy Feldman
Photographed by Sabina Louise Pierce

BOWTIE
PRESS®

Lead Editor: Amy Deputato
Associate Editor: Jennifer Calvert
Design Manager: Véronique Bos
Production Supervisor: Jessica Jaensch
Assistant Production Manager: Tracy Vogtman
Book Project Specialist: Karen Julian

Vice President, Chief Content Officer: June Kikuchi
Vice President, Kennel Club Books: Andrew DePrisco
BowTie Press: Jennifer Calvert, Amy Deputato, Lindsay Hanks,
Karen Julian, Jarelle S. Stein

The contents and subject matter within this book were created and published to provide accurate and reliable information to the reader. While every reasonable precaution has been taken in preparation of this book, neither the publisher nor the author shall be liable for any adverse effects arising from the use or application of the subject matter contained herein. The recipes and suggestions provided within this cookbook are to be used at the reader's discretion and risk and only after consultation with a veterinarian.

A Division of BowTie, Inc.
3 Burroughs, Irvine, CA 92618

Library of Congress Cataloging-in-Publication Data
Feldman, Kathryn Levy.
    The culinary canine : great chefs cook for their dogs and so can you! / written by Kathryn Levy Feldman ; photographs by Sabina Louise Pierce.
        p. cm.
    ISBN 978-1-935484-56-1
    1. Dogs--Food--Recipes. I. Title.
    SF427.4.F45 2011
    636.7'085--dc22
                            2011012346

Printed and bound in China
17 16 15 14 13 12 11   1 2 3 4 5 6 7 8 9 10

Dedication

To the two- and
four-legged members
of my family,
with love and
thanks for always
being there.
—KLF

To my "mini-me,"
Maddie, who
inspired this book
with her good taste!
—SLP

Contents

Preface

At a glance, a cookbook for dogs may seem like another example of our growing propensity to share everything human with our beloved canines. In a nation in which approximately 46 million households own dogs and spend over $45 billion taking care of them, the lines of demarcation between what is meant for Fred and what is fine for Fido are increasingly blurred. According to Bob Vetere, president of the American Pet Products Association, because of our growing tendency to humanize our pets, the disparity in the quality of our lives and theirs is rapidly disappearing. From clothing to chemotherapy, from birthday parties to kidney transplants, nothing seems to be too good, or too expensive, for our "best friends."

Nowhere is this more apparent than in the aisles of your local pet-supply store, where "all natural," "organic," and even "human-grade" are on the labels that grace the packages of foods made of everything from beef to lamb to duck to soy to sweet potatoes. However, after the national pet-food recall of 2007 (the largest pet-food recall in history, according to the Veterinary Information Network), in which melamine-laced pet food was linked to the deaths and illnesses of thousands of cats and dogs, many pet owners began to cook their own dog food.

Our intention is not to weigh in on the pros and cons of this practice or to become enmeshed in the discussion of what is and what is not considered to be "nutritionally balanced." However, we couldn't help noticing that the concept of taking control of our food—knowing where it comes from, how it is cultivated, and how it is prepared—has become important for all members of the family. Perhaps it was after watching an episode of *Top Chef*, or maybe it was after reading another list of "Top Ten Places to Get Thin Crust Pizza," but the question of what professional chefs feed their dogs began to simmer in our minds. We truly had no idea what we would find, but we were curious enough to begin asking.

Preface

It turns out that the concept of recording what people feed their dogs is far from a modern obsession. As far back as the sixteenth century, English poet George Turberville was writing "recipes" for his working hounds, providing instructions for combining certain ingredients in specific proportions to cure canine conditions. His cure for "common mange," found in *The Noble Art of Venerie or Hunting* (1575), calls for two handfuls of wild herbs, including sorrel leaves, to be boiled in lye and vinegar, strained, mixed with "grey soap," and rubbed all over the dogs for four or five days.

By 1782, Peter Beckford had recorded, in the second edition of his book *Peter Beckford's Thoughts on Hunting*, a recipe for dog food that included oatmeal mixed with horsemeat. "Oatmeal, I believe, makes the best meat for hounds; barley is certainly the cheapest. . . If mixed, an equal quantity of each, it will then do very well, but barley alone will not," he wrote. In 1893, Joseph Franklin Perry, writing under the pseudonym Ashmont, devoted the first five substantial chapters of his tome, *Kennel Secrets: How to Breed, Exhibit and Manage Dogs*, to the dietary needs of dogs from birth to old age. In fact, his general recommendations sound remarkably contemporary: "The dog can safely be regarded as capable of digesting and assimilating vegetables as well as animal foods, and considering his race, generally the conclusion must be reached that whatever may have been the food of his ancestors, a varied and mixed diet now best suits his requirements."

Today's chefs use many of the same ingredients that Beckford and Ashmont employed, including the aforementioned oatmeal, vegetables, and various forms of meat. Some of the recipes, including those of Geraldine Gilliland, Marc Penvenne, and Karyn Calabrese, are the actual recipes that they use to feed their dogs on a daily basis. Others, such as those of Amaryll Schwertner, Eli Zabar, and Matthew Levin, are meant to be combined with high-quality dry dog food. The majority of the recipes, however, are meant to be "special-occasion" meals—a sort of canine equivalent of what you might enjoy if you frequented one of the establishments in which these talented chefs cook for their customers.

What all of the recipes have in common is that each one has been prepared with great love. So, as modern as this book seems, what it truly demonstrates is our unabashed, perennial affection for the dogs who share our lives. *Bon appétit!*

Acknowledgments

While too many cooks may spoil the broth, the opposite is true when it comes to creating a book "from scratch." We could not have combined these ingredients in any palatable form without the assistance of many helpers, both in and out of the kitchen. One of the most important things we learned is that at the intersection of dogs and food are fabulous people, and we are grateful beyond measure to all of them for their contributions to this project.

First and foremost, we thank all of the chefs in this book, many of whom have been loyal to this project since its inception many moons ago. We thank you for sharing your dogs, your culinary talents, and your recipes with us. We were not underfed! We also extend our thanks to all of the public-relations people, most of whom are dog lovers themselves, who put us in contact with these amazing chefs. They kept us supplied with a steady stream of talent. We appreciate everyone who gave us leads on suitable candidates and all of our Help a Reporter Out (HARO) responders. We're especially grateful to Peter Shankman for HARO, a fabulous resource.

We offer our sincere thanks to Patty Khuly for writing an amazing introduction to this book, for testing the recipes, and for her overall devotion to the cause. If there ever were a more multitalented veterinarian, we certainly have never met him or her, nor have we ever met anyone more suited to be our voice of authority. We also thank Elizabeth Tobey and the amazing staff at the National Sporting Library in Virginia for their invaluable assistance in researching the history of dog keeping.

We are grateful to all the people at BowTie Press who believed in this project and nurtured it until it was cooked to perfection; to our families and friends for sustaining us with their love, friendship, and belief in what we were doing; to our devoted four-legged companions for always being there; and to the spirit of Barbaro for bringing us together and inspiring us to never give up.

—*Kit and Sabina*

Introduction

by Patty Khuly, VMD, MBA

I've always said it. Despite my choice of professions, I'm decidedly a foodie first. While it's hard to say which came first, my lifelong interest in both the culinary arts and animal science were never too far apart. Indeed, they're now so intertwined that it makes me wonder how I didn't catch the connection sooner.

Sure, keeping a flock of healthy, hilarious hens might've been more than enough to prove that veterinary medicine and foodism go hand in hand. But when you add in a couple of goats and all the milk and cheese that portends, is it not obvious that my professional know-how craves exploitation by the foodie within? Or is it vice versa?

Yes, it only stands to reason, with all of this animal protein in abundance and foodist drive in evidence, that I might want to cook for my dogs. And you would be right. Like you probably do, I find that cooking for my nonhuman family is a rewarding, creative undertaking with which I can get obsessed at times.

And why not? Food preparation is more than an occasional rainy Sunday afternoon endeavor. For people like us, it's a lifestyle choice.

In this age of frenetic foods and prepackaged convenience, where kitchen appliances seem cynically designed to last no more than three Thanksgivings, and dump-and-stir cooking shows can be mindlessly consumed via the video device of your choosing, is it any wonder that some of us want to reprise our ancestors' more intimate ways with food?

And given that our pets—dogs in particular—seem to have played their domesticated companion-animal chess game to Darwin's delight, does it not stand to reason that their pet-in-the-bed role should extend to our homes' hearths?

Braised lamb and glazed pastry? It's not just for humans anymore. It's for anyone you're willing to consider family. Increasingly, that designation includes dogs. Makes sense to me. But then (as you doubtless are aware if you're reading this), I'm smitten.

At the time of this writing, my dogged life includes Vincent, Slumdog, Pinky, and Gaston. Supporting this foursome in the lifestyle to which they've become accustomed means a seven-day-a-week cooking habit—which, lucky for them, I happen to possess.

Yet even if your household doesn't teem with spoiled, hungry mouths and your culinary repertoire barely surpasses the demands of the lowly boiled egg, let me now attempt to convince you: cooking for dogs is for you!

Here's my five-point pitch, which I'll deliver in my combined capacity as veterinarian and embarrassingly indefatigable foodie:

1. **"People" food? There is no such thing!** Food is for our dogs, too. As co-recipients of the classification "omnivore," they deserve to share in the bounty that graces our human tables.

2. **Variety is what it's all about.** More recipes, more ingredients, more better.

3. **One bag for life? Can that possibly be best?** Though commercial dog foods are "proven" to be 100-percent nutrient-balanced, such findings reflect only the current state of our animal science, such as it is. After all, if science on human

nutrition remains in dispute despite extensive research, how can we expect veterinary medicine's relatively minuscule body of evidence to have attained loftier goals? These dishes (and the book in general), as I see it, are part of a more enlightened canine lifestyle that dispenses with the "one-bag-for-life" dogma we've been trained to believe.

4. **Many pets require specialized diets that may require home cooking.** While there are commercial foods available for most health problems, veterinary nutritionists can help you devise supplementary meals or entire diets themselves to complement your pets' treatment regimen. (See the American Academy of Veterinary Nutrition's website [www.aavn.org] for more information on individualized nutrition consultations.)

5. **Not a big cook? Sensitive about your skills?** Cooking for your pets is the best way I can think of to become engaged in the kitchen. You may never achieve culinary nirvana or Chef-Perrier-style perfection (I wish), but you will likely be swayed by the sweet mysteries of the stove top into more time at the hearth on behalf of your family.

As for the recipes that follow, I can promise you that I've read through every one to ensure basic canine edibility (and, in my best estimation, palatability). And while, thus far, my kitchen hasn't taken them all on, those that have made it onto my stove or into my oven and fridge have proved not only doable, but—at least from my dogs' point of view—foolproof.

Introduction

Though none of the recipes can claim to offer a 100 percent nutritionally balanced diet, neither am I a stickler for a 100 percent home-cooked regimen. Who doesn't dine out or order in for convenience sometimes? And as for my personal pets? With my busy lifestyle, it only makes sense to serve them a rotating regimen of the kind of high-quality commercial fare now available nationwide. (Choose wisely!)

My recipe preferences? Can I help it if I'm especially attracted to the recipes I'd happily feed myself? After all, when both humans and animals can share in the benefits of a deliberate, slowly prepared, lovingly home-cooked meal, there's something almost magical that happens after the soothing labors.

Even if the enjoyment of the task doesn't exactly overwhelm you, I can promise you that the health benefits of freshness, ingredient safety, and variety alone are worth the effort. Still, for me, this knowledge is only a teensy bit more satisfying than these meals themselves. The recipes here...they're just that good.

Enjoy!

Note: *Warnings about the adverse gastrointestinal effects of a varied canine diet are typically overblown. Concessions for making significant dietary changes are easily achieved. Veterinary advice on this subject is available through your pet's own healthcare provider.*

Patty Khuly, VMD, MBA is in private veterinary practice in Miami, Florida. According to PetMD, her daily blog, FullyVetted (at www.petmd.com/blogs/fullyvetted), is the most popular veterinary-authored blog in the world, based on the number of hits received every month relative to others in the same category. She also writes for *USA Today*, the *Miami Herald*, the *Bark*, and *Veterinary Practice News*, and she wrote the foreword for the best-selling book *Homer's Odyssey* by Gwen Cooper. Homer, the cat, was Dr. Khuly's patient.

Cosme Aguilar
and Henry

**Executive Chef/
Part Owner**

● Bar Henry

New York,
New York

The Culinary Canine

Ten years ago, Manhattan native and real estate investor Winston Kulok wandered into an antiques shop in Hudson, New York. What caught his eye were the youngest items in the store—a few absolutely arresting Maltese puppies. "They were all fabulous, but one was clearly a champion," the affable restaurateur recounts. When he learned that the puppies were indeed for sale, Winston realized that he didn't have any cash to pay for his chosen champ. "I told the woman to hold him for me," he says. Winston drove back to the city, retrieved some money, and turned around to claim the puppy. "When she gave him to me, the owner cried and warned me that he might get carsick," he recalls. Henry (named after Henry Hudson) did no such thing. He sat on Winston's lap the entire way home and firmly wedged himself into Winston's heart.

It was no surprise, then, that when Winston and his wife, Carole Bergman, decided to go into the restaurant business in 2001, they chose the winsome Henry as their muse. Their first venture was a small café named Café Henri in Greenwich Village, and they joined forces with executive chef Cosme Aguilar. Cosme moved to New York in 1998 from Chiapas, Mexico, where his culinary training took place under the watchful eyes of his mother, who was known as one of the town's best cooks. In fact, Cosme, his brother, and his sister all were her apprentices, especially when she prepared elaborate meals for special neighborhood celebrations. The free-roaming dogs in town were also fed well by Cosme and his animal-loving family.

Once in New York, Cosme fell in love with French cooking, influenced no doubt by his jobs at Le Solex, Orsay, and Les Deux Gamins, all well-known and highly regarded French restaurants. It was during his eight-year tenure at Les Deux Gamins as both chef and general manager, however, that Cosme began to make his mark as one of New York's most creative chefs. It was also there that he met and eventually partnered with Winston.

Always inspired by Henry, their first venture was Café Henri in the West Village, followed by its sister location in Long Island City, and now Bar Henry, also in the Village. If Café Henri represents Henry's French alter ego, then Bar Henry, opened in 2009—with its rich copper ceiling and bar top, antique brass lighting,

black-and-white marble tile floor, and stunning 1890s bar—is his "old New York" incarnation. The menu, according to Cosme, is "American bistro" with his own unique twist, including a subtle French influence.

As for Henry, well, he is loved by everyone—especially by Cosme, who regards him as much more than the team mascot and good-luck charm. "How could you not love Henry?" Cosme wonders. Henry's personality, energy, and inquisitive, knowing gaze (as well as the unconditional love he showers on everyone) make him one of the most valuable team members! "It feels good to see his photo over the bar as I walk into work every day," says Cosme, who admits to sneaking samples to Henry. "Henry knows where to come for treats as well as a good belly rub. We've known each other for a long time."

"All of the people involved in our restaurants are family," Winston elaborates. "It comes from a feeling that Henry personifies."

Henry's Organic Chicken

Chef Cosme says, "With the chicken, Henry enjoys raw, organic diced carrots and raw, organic sugar snap peas. Sliced organic watermelon makes a lovely dessert." He uses all organic ingredients in this recipe, which makes one serving for a dog Henry's size.

INGREDIENTS
1 carrot
1 parsnip
1 celery stalk
4 cups chicken broth
6-ounce chicken breast

DIRECTIONS
Place the vegetables in a pot with the 4 cups of chicken broth. Bring to a boil and add the vegetables. Let simmer for 20 minutes.

Add the chicken and cook for 8 minutes.

Remove the chicken, cool, and slice into bite-sized pieces.

Serve with a little broth.

Karyn Calabrese

and Mitchell Howard Scherer ("Mitch")

Owner/Culinary Director

- Karyn's Raw Café and Inner Beauty Center

- Karyn's Cooked

- Karyn's on Green

- Karyn's at Home

Chicago, Illinois

Karyn Calabrese has created a raw and vegan holistic-food empire in Chicago, all of which grew out of her allergies to, as she puts it, "everything known to man." A grandmother of two, she looks twenty years younger than she is, a feat that she attributes to her "99.9 percent" raw-food diet. "Raw food is the way God intended every animal (with two or four legs) on the planet to eat," she says simply. Karyn believes that it is not enough to simply eat live foods; we also have to cleanse ourselves of the processed and cooked foods that are still in our bodies. "Any foods that aren't raw and organic tax our digestive systems," she elaborates. "The standard American diet is heavy in refined flour, sugar, and chemicals that wreak havoc on our bodies. Optimal health is all about the enzymes. There is an enzyme activity for every metabolic function in your body. Eating a raw-food diet that is rich in living enzymes eases the pressure in your digestive system so you don't age prematurely, you don't get sick, and you don't get fat."

Karyn began to spread the word about the benefits of raw food in 1981, beginning with a small group of people in her home. In 1995, she opened her first storefront, Karyn's Fresh Corner, where she taught detoxification classes, met with individual clients, and ran a raw-food café. In 2002, she combined her restaurant and holistic spa and therapy center under one roof when she opened her 7,000-square-foot raw-food/wellness emporium, Karyn's Raw Café and Inner Beauty Center. The underlying message of all of her ventures is about lifestyle choices: "If you don't take care of your body, the most magnificent machine you'll ever be given, where will you live?"

From the day it opened in 1995, when it was only the second raw-food restaurant in the country, Karyn's Raw Café, which features fresh, delicious, gourmet, raw, vegan meals, has been a Chicago hot spot and must-see destination for people from around the world, regardless of their dietary practices. The kitchen operates without a grill, oven, microwave, or other source of heat. "We don't fire any of our food," Karyn explains. "We dehydrate [it], which gives you a sense of cooking."

At Karyn's Cooked and Karyn's on Green, there are ovens—ovens from which hip, gourmet vegan meals emerge daily, challenging many to question whether they are truly eating vegan fare. Karyn's veggie chili has all of Chicago talking, and her Mexican food is legendary. "The cooked restaurants provide a bridge for people who are transitioning to an all-raw diet so they don't feel a loss," she says. "[It's] a journey, and it doesn't happen overnight." For those who are too busy to dine out, Karyn's At Home prepares a week's worth of raw or cooked vegan meals that can be picked up at the café or delivered to your door. "You don't have to be a vegan to love my food!" she proclaims. "I'm making veganism sexy."

The former actress and model has made numerous appearances on the *Oprah Winfrey Show* and, together with Oprah, received the prestigious First Annual Raw and Living Foods Golden Branch Award in 2000 by the International Raw & Living Foods Association. The award, which comes with the title "Raw Foodist of the Year," was in recognition of the pair's significant contribution to the raw-food

movement of introducing the idea of raw and living foods to the greatest number of people in the mainstream public.

Karyn's philosophy of "eating the way God intended" extends to her beloved chocolate Miniature Poodle, Mitchell Howard (her husband's middle name) Scherer (her married name)—better known as "Mitch"—for whom she even plunges her hands into raw lamb. "I haven't eaten meat for over forty years," she notes, "so you know this is true love." The devotion works both ways, as Mitch rarely leaves

her side. "I call him a little boy in a dog suit," she confesses. "If someone in one of my classes doesn't like Mitch, I suggest [that he or she] leave." The pair practices agility training two times a week ("He's such a little genius; he knows the course," she gushes), and Mitch has had the same "nanny" his whole life for when Karyn is out of town. "He is never alone," she states emphatically.

Mitch auditioned for the television show *America's Top Dog*, even though Karyn knew that if he were selected, they would never have the time to participate. "When I heard that the producers were coming to Chicago, I called them and said, 'I don't want to be on your show, but you just have to see this dog,'" she explains. During the audition, Karyn told Mitch the name of each of the producers and then told him to bring something to the one named Judy. "He did it, and they were floored," she laughs.

The bond that Karyn and Mitch share even extends to their respective behaviors. "We're both high maintenance and we don't like to have our heads touched," she confesses. "I am the ultimate dog lover."

Raw Dog Food

Chef Karyn says, "Because all living animals are meant to survive on whole, enzymatically rich, raw foods, not only will our pets survive but they also will thrive like their jungle counterparts without the diseases so common to domesticated pets (and humans) who eat cooked foods. This recipe is what I feed Mitch pretty much exclusively, with variations based on the type of meat. It will take less of this mixture to feed and fill your pet than what you are currently feeding him. In general, a portion size will be about 2 percent of your dog's weight, so a 25-pound dog would get half a pound of the food, which is what Mitch gets twice a day."
Dr. Khuly's note: *"For the squeamish, this is a great recipe that can also be served cooked."*

INGREDIENTS

4 or 5 servings of seasonal vegetables/fruits, organic when possible. Options include:

- 1 small apple
- 1 small pear
- 1 small squash
- 2 or 3 carrots
- 2 or 3 celery stalks
- 1 small sweet potato
- 1 bunch kale
- 1 bunch romaine lettuce
- 1 cup bean or alfalfa sprouts
- 1 cup green beans

1 Tbsp kelp
1 Tbsp molasses or honey
1 Tbsp Karyn's Green Meal Powder or another powdered green superfood (available at health-food stores)
¼ cup apple-cider vinegar
2 eggs, shells included
1 Tbsp lecithin granules
1 tsp powdered vitamin C (optional)

Approximately 2 pounds of any of the following raw meats, ideally including organ meats, from your butcher:

- chicken (including necks)
- lamb
- beef
- bison
- turkey
- buffalo
- fish (be careful of bones)

DIRECTIONS

Process the vegetables and fruits in a food processor; they can be pureed or left in chunks, depending on your dog's preference. Add the kelp, molasses or honey, green powdered superfood, vinegar, eggs, lecithin, and vitamin C (optional) to the food processor.

Bag and freeze individual portions of the vegetable/fruit mixture for your dog. When you serve the food, the proportion should be 75 percent meat to 25 percent vegetable/fruit, so measure out and freeze your portion sizes based on these numbers. For example, a 12-ounce meal should comprise 9 ounces of meat and 3 ounces of vegetable/fruit mixture.

Divide the meat into single servings depending on your dog's size, weight, and daily activity. If you are using organ meats, they should account for 50 percent of the meat serving. Freeze the meat portions in individual plastic bags. Thaw portions before serving.

Steve Chiappetti

and Maggie and Rocky

Executive Chef

- Viand

Chicago,
Illinois

There is literally no aspect of the food industry with which Chef Steve Chiappetti, a native of Chicago's South Side, has not been involved. From butchery to baking to food photography and styling, he has truly done it all. His family name is on Chicago's oldest slaughter- and packinghouse, Chiappetti Lamb and Veal, which is the last remaining slaughterhouse in the Chicago stockyards. "There is a room in the Chicago Historical Museum devoted to my family," he laughs. And while his track record of restaurant establishments is every bit as historical, he does admit that he was fired from his first job at a local McDonald's, where he was told that he might not be cut out for the business!

With an Italian father and a French mother, Steve grew up absorbing a world of food cultures, which he translated into his own unique style of cooking with a mixture of formal training and hands-on experience. He attended culinary school at Kendall College and has worked for some of the biggest names in the business, including Chef Fernand Gutierrez at the Ritz-Carlton's The Dining Room and Chef Paul Bartolotta at Spiaggia. He represented the United States in the Bocuse d'Or, one of Europe's most prestigious food competitions, and was nominated for the James Beard Foundation's Rising Star Chef Award in 1997.

Steve opened a string of highly successful Chicago restaurants, including Mango, Grapes, and Rhapsody, the latter of which is a three-star contemporary bistro adjacent to the Chicago Symphony. "I opened five restaurants and a culinary school in five years," he reminisces. "I worked seven days a week." On January 1, 2000, he sold everything and took some time off. It was then that he dabbled in food photography, showing his work in several galleries; wrote a cookbook, *The Hauser Diet*, with Dr. Ross Hauser; developed his own line of dried spices; opened a bakery, a classic French bistro, and a fudge shop; and began consulting for White Lodging, a prominent developer, owner, and manager in the hospitality industry.

At Viand, which he developed in conjunction with White Lodging, Steve says that he is "reinventing and reinterpreting a lot of classics and favorites. I love to make dishes that are new and familiar at the same time."

Steve and his wife, Leslie, feel strongly about supporting the efforts of local community organizations, which is how they found themselves, one afternoon, on the campus of Lamb's Farm, a nonprofit residential and vocational community of adults with developmental disabilities in Libertyville, Illinois. "The residents of Lamb's Farm run all sorts of businesses on their campus, including a bakery, a country store, a thrift shop, and an inn," explains Leslie. "They were having an open house, and there happened to be some puppies for sale. As soon as we saw Maggie, a Chihuahua mix, who was all of six weeks old, we knew we had found our dog! She was so excited and super-energetic. We wanted a small, playful puppy who would play with us and our kids."

Rocky, a Chihuahua/Shiba Inu mix, joined their family about two years later. "Rocky was rescued from a shelter by an acquaintance with good intentions," says Leslie. "Unfortunately, Rocky did not get along with her cats. She asked if I might be interested in him, and as soon as I took one look at him, with that snaggletooth and one ear up, I knew I had to have him."

The Culinary Canine

The two dogs are the perfect snuggle companions to everyone in the family ("They manage to put themselves into a crevice wherever we sit," laughs Leslie) and have turned out to be inseparable. "When they sleep, they curl up like yin and yang," notes Steve. "From behind, you can't tell who is who; they are so much in sync. They are very respectful of each other's spaces, and when they eat, one sits and waits for the other to finish. They even alternate who gets to eat first."

One of the family's favorite things to do with the dogs is take them to a forest preserve to hike. "They keep up with us and usually stay very close by—unless there is a squirrel," smiles Leslie. "Rocky climbs halfway up a tree to chase a squirrel. It's like he has springs on the backs of his legs!"

When it comes to cooking for the dogs, Steve actually has a lot of practice. While he worked at the Ritz-Carlton, it was one of his responsibilities to cook for the dogs of famous guests. "Hooch [a Dogue de Bordeaux named Beasley] stayed there when he was filming the movie *Turner and Hooch* with Tom Hanks," Steve says. "I used to prepare 5 pounds of smoked turkey a day just for him!"

Pet Patties

Chef Steve says, "Maggie and Rocky stand by the stove when I am cooking this and wait patiently for their dinner." This recipe makes six patties, and Steve serves one patty per meal to each of his 7-pound dogs.

INGREDIENTS
½ pound boneless, skinless chicken breast
1 peeled carrot
3 strips double-smoked bacon
½ clove garlic
1 tsp ground cumin
Dash ground coriander
Dash paprika
Dash salt
Dash pepper
1 egg
1 Tbsp olive oil
2 slices cheddar cheese

DIRECTIONS
Using a stand mixer with a food grinder attachment (medium-hole plate, if you have the restaurant version), grind the chicken, carrot, and bacon together. In the bowl of the mixer, add the spices and egg to the ground ingredients and mix everything completely.

Form golf-ball-sized patties and flatten them to a ½-inch thickness. Set the patties on a plate.

Preheat a nonstick pan with the olive oil on medium heat. Cook the patties until well done and browned on each side. Add the cheese on top of the patties at the end of cooking, keeping the patties over the heat until the cheese is slightly melted.

Cool for about 10 minutes before serving.

Dominique Crenn

and Maximus

Chef/Owner

- Atelier Crenn

San Francisco,
California

The Culinary Canine

The city and the country have both left their impression on Chef Dominique Crenn. Growing up in Versailles, France, the daughter of a politician whose best friend was a food critic, Dominique developed a sophisticated palate at an early age. In fact, when Dominique was about eight years old, she told her mother, who introduced her to cooking, that she wanted to be one of the top chefs in the world. She also credits the summers spent on her grandparents' farm in Brittany, picking vegetables and milking cows, for inspiring her passion for organic, sustainable, local produce.

It looks like Dominique has achieved her dream. Having competed on the popular Food Network show *The Next Iron Chef* in 2009, and having beaten Iron Chef Michael Symon in "Battle Yogurt" on *Iron Chef America* in 2010, Dominique has proven that she can more than hold her own with any toque in the world. "You know, it is tough even now for a woman in France to become a top chef," she notes. "It is still not an industry in which women are readily accepted." Not so in the United States, especially in San Francisco, where Dominique makes her home.

In 1988, after traveling extensively throughout Europe to learn the cooking styles and ingredients of many cultures and earning her bachelor's degree in international business from the Academy of International Commerce of Paris, Dominique moved to San Francisco and fell in love with the city. She trained under some of the best chefs in the business, including Jeremiah Tower and Mark Franz, before making her mark at such well-known eateries as Campton Place, 2223 Market, the Park Hyatt Grill, and the Yoyo Bistro. Dominique took Indonesia by storm in 1997, when she moved there to become the country's first female executive chef in her position at the InterContinental Jakarta MidPlaza hotel. Her time in Jakarta was cut short by the region's political unrest, and in 1998 she returned to the States, where she soon took the executive chef position at the Manhattan Country Club in Manhattan Beach, California. There, she catered private parties for club members, including celebrities such as Juliette Binoche, Sidney Poitier, Sharon Stone, and Cyndi Lauper, as well as national and international political figures, including Al Gore. A stint at Abode in Santa Monica followed in 2007.

San Francisco beckoned once again, and Dominique returned in late 2007 to head Luce in the InterContinental San Francisco hotel. She earned the restaurant a coveted Michelin star in October 2009. In fact, Luce was named one of the twenty "Best New Restaurants" by *Esquire* magazine in November 2008 and was selected by *Robb Report* editors as one of seven restaurants named "Best of the Best" for 2009, and Dominique earned her own accolades as *Esquire*'s "Chef of the Year" for 2008.

While still in charge at Luce, Dominique opened Atelier Crenn in January 2011 in honor of her father, an artist who had a painting studio in the Brittany region of France. *Atelier* means "workshop" in French, and her father's artwork graces the restaurant's walls. The restaurant is a small (forty seats in the front plus an intimate private dining room in the back), seasonally driven, very European-style venue where guests can create their own menus based on a list of about fifteen

courses. The wine list changes monthly, and, one Sunday evening each month, the restaurant is closed and the kitchen is reserved for members of the industry. All of Dominique's friends in the restaurant business gather in the kitchen and cook for each other. As of April 1, 2011, Dominique was no longer associated with Luce, while Atelier Crenn continued to rack up praise from national and international press.

Dominique rescued her Chihuahua, Maximus, as a companion to her late Chihuahua, Julius, about four years ago. "It was love at first sight on my part, even though he was so tiny and very shaky and scared, having been abandoned in Oakland," she recalls. "But we had a sleepover; he played with Julius and seemed to fit in. He is just a little man, like Julius was, not a typical snappy Chihuahua. A little man with a special soul."

Since Julius passed away, Maximus "continues to find his own identity." "He's

become a really cool dog. Each and every moment with him is the best. We dialogue together and learn something new every day about each other," Dominique smiles. "He is a special soul, an extension of my heart, and I know that he is happy even when I am working long hours. I take him everywhere with me when I am free. In that way, we are a perfect match."

A passionate advocate of using organic, sustainable ingredients, Dominique applies the same philosophy to how she feeds her pets. "No one should eat processed things," she says adamantly. To that end, Maximus "probably eats better than most people," and blueberries are one of his favorite foods. "I couldn't live my life without my dog," Dominique reflects.

Maximus's Poached Chicken, Organic Brown Rice, and Blueberries

Chef Dominique says, "Maximus loves blueberries! This recipe is made with only the finest ingredients because he deserves the best."

INGREDIENTS
1 pound organic chicken breast, skinless and boneless
4½ cups organic chicken stock
1½ cups brown rice
3 medium organic carrots, peeled
6 blueberries

DIRECTIONS
In one saucepan, poach the chicken in the chicken stock until tender. In another saucepan, cover the brown rice with water and let it cook slowly.

Juice two carrots and slice the other one. Then, in a third saucepan, cook the carrot slices in the carrot juice until soft.

Drain the carrots and add them to the brown rice. Cut the chicken into small pieces and add it to the rice and carrots.

Mix and let cool. Place the mixture into the dog's bowl; top with blueberries before serving.

Et voilà!

Roberta Deen

and Dobbie, Chica, and Bella Luna

Chef/Owner

- Capers Catering

Los Angeles,
California

The Culinary Canine

The opportunity to create a catering company with a friend lured Roberta Deen out of the classroom, where she had been teaching kindergarten and first grade, and into the kitchen. That was in 1975, and she has never looked back. That Los Angeles catering company, Along Came Mary, is still going strong and is known as the go-to caterer for many of those on Hollywood's A-list. In 1986, Roberta decided to launch her own, more intimate, boutique catering company, Capers Catering. Roberta's clients still include many of the "rich and famous," especially those who prefer to keep a lower profile.

A self-taught chef, Roberta "got the best training in the world working as a food tester for *Bon Appétit* magazine between 1980 and 1990." "The program was designed to use professional cooks to test the recipes in a home setting," she recounts. "[This was] a fine idea to ensure that the recipes would work for the home cook, but Los Angeles is a big city. We would grill quail and rush across town, praying that it would still be edible! We would finish it up in the microwave or on an electric stovetop and hold our breath while the tasters would gather in the tiny kitchen and taste. The comments were deadly serious, which was all the more incongruous since the contents of the magazine were being decided by the equivalent of a culinary Pony Express!"

Ultimately, *Bon Appétit* did build its own test kitchen, where Roberta did get to work for a few years until the editors moved the entire program in-house. She will always be grateful for that opportunity to learn from the best. "It was an amazing time and opportunity," she says. "I met most of the great chefs who were changing the face of food in California, and I learned what will work and what will not. I will always be grateful to my friends, Meg McComb (former pastry chef for Valentino's and owner of Meg's on Rodeo) and Lynn Willmott (former Along Came Mary chef), who made it possible for me to get the testing job, and to my program mentors for the best culinary education one could hope for."

Capers Catering has provided Roberta with endless opportunities to perfect the techniques and recipes she tested at *Bon Appétit* as well as create hundreds of her own. She is known for using only the freshest and finest ingredients and for her expertise in designing menus that convey a sense of discovery and excitement. Whether it is an intimate dinner for two or a backyard barbecue for a thousand, Roberta never skimps on quantity or quality and supplies everything that every host or hostess needs or wants.

There have always been dogs in Roberta's life, but not until Dobbie, a rescued Cocker Spaniel, did she own one who required a special diet. It was Dobbie's groomer, in fact, who suspected that the Cocker might be allergic to the wheat products, gluten, and fillers in what Roberta notes was "the very good and expensive prescription dog food we had been feeding him." The clues were Dobbie's dry, flaky skin; lethargy; dull coat; and water retention. Within a few months of switching Dobbie to a pure, organic, wild-salmon-based dry dog food with no fillers, Roberta reports that she had her "beautiful, active Dobbie back." "Dobbie loves his kibble, but today he wants to play more than he wants to eat," she continues. "He is like a puppy again and has even lost a few pounds."

The Culinary Canine

Roberta has learned to be especially creative when it comes to cooking for Dobbie. "Treat time was out of the question for a while," she says. "There were few gluten-free treats on the market, so I went to work developing Puppy Pâté especially for celiac dogs." In fact, the treats are a big hit with Dobbie as well as with Chica, Roberta's Chihuahua/Chinese Crested mix, and Bella Luna, a Manchester Terrier who Roberta calls her "soul mate." "Even when given a choice between homemade and store-bought, Dobbie, Chica, and Bella love their Puppy Pâté best," she smiles. Dobbie is living proof that a switch in diet can be life-changing.

Puppy Pâté en Plastique

Chef Roberta says, "The en plastique *technique was taught by John Sedlar in a wonderful class given at the famous Ma Maison restaurant in Los Angeles. Somehow I never got around to using it until I created the Puppy Pâté for our celiac Cocker Spaniel, Dobbie....You can vary the size of the rolls to suit your dog's size and preference. You can serve the pâté warm if you are using it as a full meal; the size of the serving will depend on the size of your dog. Alternatively, you can break up the slices and use them as training treats."*

Dr. Khuly's note: *"Puppy Pâté en Plastique is magnificent! It worked great for me, but I found it easier to form the sausages once all of the chopped mixture was very cold."*

INGREDIENTS

1½ pounds boneless, skinless raw salmon filet, diced into 1-inch pieces

3 Tbsp dried parsley flakes or 6 Tbsp chopped fresh parsley, curly or Italian

1–2 large raw carrots, finely diced

3 large eggs

Optional: raw peas, broccoli, string beans, zucchini, or other dog-friendly veggies, finely diced

DIRECTIONS

Place all ingredients in a food processor. Using the metal blade, pulse to blend and chop finely, but not until completely smooth. Transfer the mixture into a bowl. *Optional:* Cover the bowl with plastic wrap and refrigerate for at least 2–3 hours. The chilling will make it easier to form the sausages.

Place a piece of plastic wrap about 18 inches wide by 18 inches long on a work surface. Spoon about one-third of the mixture onto the plastic film along the edge nearest you, forming a "sausage" of about 1½ inches in diameter and about 6 inches in length. Using the film to help you, roll the salmon pâté up to form a log.

Twist the ends of the film to form a tight seal. Cut two more pieces of film, each about 9 inches long by 2 inches wide, and use them to tie off each end, close to the sausage (or use kitchen twine to tie off the ends). Repeat the entire sausage-rolling process two more times with remaining pâté.

Bring a pot of water to a rolling boil. Carefully slide the wrapped pâté logs into the boiling water and reduce the heat to a simmer. Cook, turning the rolls now and then, for about 15 minutes. The pâté will be firm to the touch. Using tongs, carefully remove the rolls from the water and place them on a plate. Refrigerate the rolls until chilled.

To serve, cut one end of the plastic open with scissors, and peel it back as you slice the pâté into rounds. Alternatively, you can peel all of the plastic off and store the log in a plastic bag.

The pâté seems to keep a long time—two weeks in the original plastic wrap and ten days if you remove the plastic wrapping—but it won't be around that long, because the puppies love it!

Geraldine Gilliland

and Rescued "Guests"

Chef/Owner

- Lula Cocina Mexicana

- Finn McCool's Irish Pub

Santa Monica, California

- Rancho Chiquita

Malibu, California

The Culinary Canine

Renowned chef, author, restaurateur, and philanthropist Geraldine Gilliland has reached the stage in her career at which she is able to combine her two great passions: food and dogs.

Since she arrived in Los Angeles from Northern Ireland in 1975, Gilliland has established herself as one of the top chefs in the country. "I always thought I'd be a schoolteacher, but I never thought I'd own restaurants!" laughs the holder of multiple degrees in classical French cuisine and home economics. Indeed, one of Geraldine's first jobs in California was teaching culinary classes at Santa Monica College as well as for UCLA's extension program. It wasn't long before first Williams-Sonoma and then Montana Mercantile hired her as a cooking instructor, and she began to work with renowned chefs around the globe.

Fast-forward to 1984, when her (now-deceased) husband, Theodore Lonsway, found a restaurant for sale in an underdeveloped area ("Actually [it was] a wasteland at the time," she corrects) in Santa Monica. The price was right, so she took the plunge. Gilliland's Café opened on August 8, 1984, to great critical and public acclaim. "People still stop me to tell me how much they loved it," she says. Lula Cocina Mexicana, decorated with original murals painted by renowned artist Eloy Torrez and artwork by George Yepes and Frank Romero, followed in 1991. In 1993, Geraldine opened Jake and Annie's, a popular American-Irish hot spot, also in Santa Monica, and then the Washington Street Bar & Grill in 1997, featuring food cooked over red oak wood from the Santa Ynez Valley. In 2001, Geraldine had her late stepfather's pub in Ireland painstakingly dismantled and shipped through the Panama Canal to California to be reconstructed. On St. Patrick's Day 2002, Finn McCool's, a true Irish pub, was opened on Main Street in Santa Monica.

Geraldine has been featured in the L.A. *Times' Fine Cooking* magazine and *Bon Appétit* magazine, the latter of which named her "one of the top six chefs in the United States." Her book, *Grills and Greens*, was nominated for a James Beard Award. In 2011, she received the California Heritage Museum Award for her support of her community and of California's Chicano art collective.

At the same time that she was opening restaurants, Geraldine began rescuing dogs. "It began with Brigid, then Bucky, Stinky, Marmalade, Carlos, Charlie, Flintstone,

Chiquita, Carmen, Goldie, Kelly, Jake, Raphael ("Rafi"), Lula, Paloma, Lucy, Sam, Roxie, George, Squeakers, Chloe, Holmes, Lilly, Rocco, Alex, Baron, Morgen, Oscar, and the latest, Ms. Coco Chanel," says Geraldine wistfully. "They all had names but needed homes. I rescued Brigid, the first one, who I found at 72 Market Street, the day we opened Gilliland's." Geraldine's late husband was a "cat guy," and long before the dogs, the couple had seven cats. Once the dogs came, everyone got along fine—until the arrival of Lula and Rafi, at which point an indoor-outdoor cat house (outdoor enclosure that was connected to the house and off-limits to the dogs) was

built at their house, in Venice at the time. When they moved to Malibu, the outdoor cat house included trees and climbing obstacles and was designed to keep the cats safe from coyotes and other predators, the elements, and their new "siblings."

As word spread about Geraldine's affinity for dogs, so did cries for help. "One day, I got a call from Diane Keaton about two black Labs who needed to be adopted together," she recalls. Ashley and Asher, whom Geraldine renamed Lula and Raphael, "never met anyone they didn't want to bite, until they met me!" she laughs. Another day, a white puppy appeared, tied up at her gate. "That was Paloma, who grew into a Great Pyrenees," she remembers. One time, two Golden Retrievers showed up in her backyard. "Roxy and Flinstone," she smiles. "We were rapidly growing out of our tiny little house in Venice! I needed more space and a proper kennel license."

This is why Rancho Chiquita, high in the Malibu hills, was so perfect. "It wasn't the house that sold me, although it was spectacular—complete with a Mexican beehive oven. It was the land," she laughs. "All I could think of was how many dogs we could save!" In addition to being Geraldine's residence, where she lives with her rescued animals, Rancho Chiquita—with its breathtaking panoramic ocean view and 250 acres of rolling hills—is a popular location for weddings, charity events, and movie shoots. Though shelters continue to call Geraldine, she is adamant that she cannot take any more than ten dogs at a time.

Today, Geraldine's culinary empire is down to two restaurants—Finn's and Lula's—as well as her beloved Rancho Chiquita, which she shares with an ever-changing array of rescued "permanent guests." In 1989, she started serving her pets a raw diet that she developed to help combat some of their allergies, and she has found it to be extremely beneficial. "I noticed that when animals kill other animals in the wild, they immediately go for the intestines. Feeding raw food seemed to make complete sense," she explains. "Lilly, the Cairn Terrier and one of the dogs for whom I started this recipe, was allergic to wheat, and Carlos, the Golden Retriever, would develop hot spots in the summer. Once I put them on a raw diet, these issues disappeared. In fact, Carlos lived to be eighteen years old and Lilly, twenty-two!"

Rancho Chiquita
Homemade Organic Dog Food

Chef Geraldine says, "Every dog at my ranch eats this food. I make it two times a week in enormous batches and refrigerate it. I do believe in this diet. My dogs do not have any allergies, and they live very long lives. They eat no dry food or bones of any kind. And since raw food is easily digested, dogs on this diet don't tend to gain weight."

INGREDIENTS

4 cups water
4 pounds fresh organic ground meat, such as beef, chicken, lamb, or turkey
4 cups pureed fresh organic vegetables (recommended vegetables include squash, carrots, and jicama; do not use nightshade vegetables such as eggplant, tomatoes, potatoes, or peppers)

Gilliland Base Mix
4 pounds rye flakes
3 pounds barley flakes
1 pound quick-cooking oat flakes
1 pound regular oat flakes
8 cups sunflower seeds
⅜ cup flax seeds
⅜ cup sesame seeds

DIRECTIONS

Combine all of the Gilliland Base Mix ingredients and store the mix in a covered, critter-safe storage container. Gilliland Base Mix can be stored for up to three months.

Place 4 cups of Gilliland Base Mix in a large pot. Add enough water to cover the dry ingredients (about 4 cups). Bring to a boil and then lower the heat and simmer for 20 minutes. Allow the mixture to cool, and then mix in the raw meat and vegetables.

Serve to your canine kids! The serving size depends on age, size, and activity level; one serving is typically 2 to 5 percent of your dog's body weight.

This recipe keeps in the refrigerator for up to four days. It freezes well but must be thawed thoroughly before serving.

Carmen González

and Jeeter

Master Chef

New York,
New York

It's very hard work running a restaurant, especially one that continually garners the industry's top honors, including *Wine Spectator*'s Award of Excellence from 2004–2006, AAA's coveted Four Diamond Award in 2005 and 2006, and a listing in the 2007 *Zagat America's Top Restaurants* guide. "You have no life," admits Carmen González, sole proprietor of the renowned Carmen the Restaurant in Coral Gables, Florida, and one of the foremost female chefs in America. "I used to get ill when a customer said he or she didn't like my food."

Loyal Miami foodies followed her from her first restaurant, the fifty-seat Clowns, which she opened in 1990 in Coral Gables (and closed when the Gulf War put a damper on business), to the Miami Club to Tamarind at the Sheraton Gateway and, finally, to Carmen the Restaurant. They may have been devastated when water damage from a fire upstairs in the David Williams Hotel forced her to close her celebrated venue, but Carmen was ready to move on. "I always wanted to come back to New York, so I did," laughs the energetic native of Puerto Rico. "Believe it or not, I'm a cold-weather person!"

At just 4 feet 11 inches tall, she is also "the biggest Yankees fan in the world." "One morning at 4 a.m., I got an email from PetFinder with Jeeter's photo," she recalls. "I took one look at him and knew immediately that he was my boy! I got my first Poodle when I was ten...I love [the breed's] personality: strong and kind, very bright, agile, and fun." When she visited him in his foster home in nearby New Jersey, her hunch was confirmed. "I walked into this house with lots of doggies running around. Yet when I sat down, he came running, jumped up on the sofa, and put his head in my lap as if to say, 'Hi, Mom. Take me home,'" she says. "I don't think I chose Jeeter as much as he chose me!" And of course, she loved his name.

Since returning to New York in 2007, Carmen has been doing a lot more than attending baseball games. She took over Lucy of Gramercy, the restaurant in ABC Carpet and Home at the time, for a brief stint, and she continues to travel to food and wine festivals around the country. In addition to appearing on the second season of *Top Chef Masters* (making it to the finals) and earning a check for $10,000 for the New York ASPCA, she has been developing and producing a bilingual television series on food and travel. She recently completed a cookbook, *Chef Carmen González Cooks Bacardi*, and is working on a series of cooking-related books for children. She was selected for the exclusive Nutrisystem Culinary Council, which comprises leading industry chefs from around the United States and acts as an advisory board to guide the weight-loss company in developing the best tasting and most appealing foods and menus. She was one of six chefs from *Top Chef Masters* who were invited to feature a dish in a new upscale cafe at the 2010 US Open tennis tournament, and she has a line of gourmet take-home foods in the works.

But that's not all! "I think my next career might be as a television personality and author," she muses. No stranger to the camera, Carmen had a weekly culinary show on Univision and was a regular on the network's top-rated morning show, *Despierta América*. She has appeared on the *Martha Stewart Show*, NBC's *Today Show*, *South Florida Today*, Food Network's *In Food Today*, and programs on MGM Latino and Televisa.

A graduate of the New York Restaurant School, Carmen grew up cooking. "I've always been in the kitchen," she laughs. "I have known since I was ten years old that I wanted to be a chef and have a restaurant." Her favorite birthday present, at age thirteen, was a pasta machine. Influenced by her mother and grandmother, both exceptional and very traditional cooks, Carmen has become known for her modern "American cuisine with a Puerto Rican flair," as she describes it. "Puerto Rican food is fairly limited but has tremendous potential," she notes. "I try to translate the food I remember from my childhood in a contemporary way. I want to cook what's closest to my heart."

Carmen has used her national attention and critical acclaim to support a variety of food-related causes. For many years, she has been involved with Share Our Strength (an organization dedicated to ending child hunger) and the James Beard Foundation (a culinary community) and has founded two nonprofit organizations based in South Florida: Chef Carmen Cooks for a Cure (which funds cancer research) and the Feeding the Mind Foundation (a culinary institute for

disadvantaged women). "I think chefs are very giving people," she comments. "It's one of the reasons we're chefs—what we are doing is giving, literally, certain pleasure to people every day. I'm extremely appreciative for the things that I have and the talent I've been given. I'd feel selfish if I didn't try to help others at least a little bit."

Carmen and Jeeter are usually on the go, exploring the many neighborhoods that make New York so exciting. "Jeeter is very active. He loves to walk and play ball," she says, "but he can also chill when I want to rest a bit. He is smart, sweet, and incredibly handsome—a lethal combination that is very hard to resist. He plays with everyone and brings tons of happiness to everyone around him. He is the best thing that ever happened to me."

Jeeter's Chicken with Rice

Chef Carmen says, "When Jeeter was younger, he had terrible stomach problems and ended up in the veterinary emergency room four times. After many tests, the vet found that Jeeter had a very slow digestive system and that some foods were too hard for him to digest. After giving him chicken and rice every time he got sick, I decided to stick with it, balancing it with the sweet potatoes and peas. He has not been sick since." Jeeter weighs 9½ pounds and eats ⅓ cup of this food three times a day; adjust the portions accordingly for your dog's size and feeding schedule.

INGREDIENTS

8 large chicken breasts, boneless and skinless
5 cups cold water
6 cups white rice, cooked
3 large sweet potatoes, roasted, peeled, and mashed
3 ⅓ cups sweet peas, steamed
½ cup extra virgin olive oil

DIRECTIONS

Place the chicken breasts and water in a large soup pot and bring to a boil over medium-high heat. Lower the fire to medium heat, and boil until the chicken breasts are fully cooked, around 20–25 minutes.

Remove the chicken breasts, reserving the chicken broth. Cut each chicken breast in half, place in a food processor, and pulse until you have reached pieces of the desired size for your pooch.

In a large mixing bowl, combine the rice, sweet potatoes, sweet peas, and chicken. Add the olive oil and mix with a rubber spatula. Add 3¾ cups of the chicken broth and mix.

Divide into pint or quart containers, cover tightly, and freeze.
The mix is good for up to twelve days.

Troy Graves

and Jackson

Executive Chef

Chicago,
Illinois

Troy Graves grew up in the Iowa farm community of Sheldon and joined the military after high school. An indirect-fire infantryman in the Army, Troy was deployed to Saudi Arabia during the Gulf War in October 1990, where he says that he "grew up very fast." "The military does that," he notes. "If you enlist at eighteen, generally by the time you are twenty, you are in charge of other people and their lives."

Upon completion of his service, Troy enrolled at Wayne State College in Nebraska to study political science. He started cooking in a local restaurant on weekends to earn some extra money. One day, he literally woke up and "realized this was what [he] wanted to do." Heeding the advice of his roommate, who had left Wayne State to enroll in the New England Culinary Institute in Vermont and told Troy that he could learn just as much by apprenticing himself out to master chefs, Troy did just that.

He moved to South Bend, Indiana, where he did an internship under Kent Buell at La Salle Grill. When Buell opened his own places in Michigan, first in New Buffalo and then in Kalamazoo, Troy tagged along. "It was under Kent that I learned how to cook," says Troy. "He is extremely talented."

In 1999, Troy decided to move to Chicago. He has developed quite a following in the Windy City since then, beginning with his eight-year stint at Meritage Café and Wine Bar, where he served as executive chef for four of those years.

In the spring of 2008, Troy opened Tallulah for owner Matt Fisher in Chicago's Lincoln Square neighborhood to acclaim from reviewers, customers, and industry bigwigs. He opened another restaurant for Fisher—Eve, in downtown Chicago—in October of the same year, and it has been generating a similar buzz. In fact, one of the accomplishments of which Troy is most proud is the fact that he opened two restaurants in one year that each received three stars from the *Chicago Tribune*. Although neither restaurant is still open (a function of the ebb and flow in the restaurant business), Troy and his brother John (also a chef) are hoping to fulfill their dream of opening their own restaurant.

In the meantime, the extra downtime for Troy has meant more time to spend with Jackson, the Viszla he owns with his girlfriend, Emily Brun. "He's a lot like

having a very attached child," Troy smiles. "Wherever we are, he is, usually with his beloved stuffed fox in his mouth. In fact, the other night I was upstairs with him when Emily came home. Jackson was halfway down the stairs to greet her when he realized that he didn't have the fox. He went back to get it so that he could meet her at the door with his fox in his mouth!"

The Viszla is an active sporting breed, and the couple has been surprised by just how much energy Jackson has. "By far, his favorite pastime is retrieving a tennis ball, which could go on all day," says Troy. Jackson also loves going to doggy day care ("Sometimes we even bring him if he doesn't have to be there," Troy admits) and is "super friendly" with the other dogs. "I fell for his cute face, and every moment with him is endearing," remarks Troy. "The other day, I was trying

to work out at home, and when I got down on the floor to do sit-ups, he sat on me! It would have been an amazing workout if I could have managed to do the curls with his body across mine, but he was more interested in making sure that I couldn't move! I gave up and took him for a walk, which is what he wanted to begin with."

When asked if he sees any correlation between his experience in the military and his current career, Troy notes the physical intensity associated with each. "Cooking is physically intense and the hours are long," he says, "yet I never consider my work to be a job. Even on a bad day, I love going to work. I truly believe that I am doing what I am supposed to do."

Peanut Butter–Banana Dog Treats

Chef Troy says, "Viszlas are prone to separation anxiety, and even though Jackson doesn't have it, we used to give him a toy with peanut butter inside to distract him when he was a puppy and we had to leave him. We were told that peanut butter was soothing, and it seemed to work. When we came home, there was never any peanut butter left, and he was pretty content! These treats are a variation on that theme."

INGREDIENTS
2 Tbsp oil
½ cup peanut butter
1 cup water
1½ cups whole-wheat flour
1½ cups white flour
⅓ cup dehydrated banana, crushed

DIRECTIONS
Preheat the oven to 350 degrees. Combine the oil, peanut butter, and water. Add the flour, a cup at a time, alternating with crushed banana pieces, until both are incorporated into a dough.

Knead the dough into a firm ball and roll it out to a ¼-inch thickness. Cut into 3- to 4-inch squares, or you can use a cookie cutter if you want to get fancy.

Place the pieces on an ungreased cookie sheet and bake at 350 degrees for 20 minutes.

This recipe makes approximately two-and-a-half dozen treats.

Todd and Ellen Gray

and August and Zeus

**Executive Chef/
Co-owner and
Co-owner**

• Equinox

Washington,
DC

Since opening Equinox in 1999, Todd and Ellen Gray have become the power couple of Washington's culinary scene. In fact, it was at Equinox that Michelle Obama celebrated her forty-fifth birthday on the same weekend that her husband was inaugurated as the nation's forty-fourth president! Chef Todd is known for his inventive interpretation of American cuisine, using only the finest and freshest local ingredients, and Ellen oversees the front of the house, staff training, marketing, and management. The Washington-area natives met when Ellen, in her job at the time as a food purveyor, encountered Todd while making a sales call. "He asked me out on a date," she recalls. "When I told him that I didn't date clients, he told me that he didn't think it would be a problem, since he wasn't going to buy anything from me!"

Todd's cooking has earned him recognition from the Restaurant Association of Metropolitan Washington in the form of its 2008 award for Fine Dining Restaurant of the Year and eight nominations for Chef of the Year, and he's been nominated five times for the James Beard Foundation's prestigious Best Chef: Mid-Atlantic award. Year after year, Equinox has been recognized with top industry honors (top ratings in the *Zagat* guide and *Wine Spectator*'s Award of Excellence six years in a row) and accolades from such respected publications and media outlets as the *Wall Street Journal*, the *New York Times*, CNN, *Southern Living*, *Town & Country*, *Gourmet*, and *Travel + Leisure*.

The Grays have appeared on various television shows and are working with the White House to help promote the Healthy Kids Initiative nationally. "Every chef in America is going to be asked to adopt a school to help make its food better," Ellen elaborates. The Grays are at the forefront of this movement, having started an agriculture program at the city's Murch Elementary School. Their son, Harrison, has developed such an interest in cooking that Todd began offering cooking and culinary-education instruction to families. The Grays also opened a community market, which they manage, in the Ronald Reagan Building and International Trade Center. The market, opened in 2009, specializes in fresh local produce.

As for dogs, Ellen's love for German Shepherds stems from the pet she had as a child, a former military dog named Missy. The couple's two German

Shepherds, August and Zeus, were both adopted from a German Shepherd rescue organization. Todd has grown to love and appreciate the breed. "It's a great breed for us, living in the city," Todd comments. "In fact, they match us pretty well—offering us sportiness and protection as well as loyalty and brains." The bond has extended to the couple's son, whom the dogs fiercely protect. "One of the best moments I ever had with Zeus was watching my then-toddler son use Zeus's tail to pull himself up to standing while Zeus patiently turned his head around and watched."

As for having a pair of male German Shepherds, Todd explains that they are so devoted to each other that "we swear they know what the other is thinking,

like an old married couple. They are, I guess you could say, 'life partners in a committed relationship.' They love each other as much as they love us. It's a big furfest going on!"

Ellen is devoted to all types of working dogs and was thrilled that Congress recently passed a law that permits civilians to adopt retired war dogs. "The waiting time is about a year, but these dogs are true heroes and well worth the wait," she says. A board member of the Washington Humane Society, Ellen also dreamed up the annual Sugar and Champagne charity event, in which the city's finest pastry chefs and wine purveyors come together to raise funds for the city's humane society. In a city with a crowded social calendar, this event seems to top everyone's list!

Pup Casserole

Chef Todd says, "Like us, our dogs live to eat. The best is coming home at night after I have walked all over the kitchen floor during service, and the soles of my shoes are licked up and down by both of them—you can see what interests them after a shift by the bottom of my shoes! I can't imagine how lucky they think I am, with all of these smells on me every night—I had to create something gourmet and special for them."

INGREDIENTS
½ cup chicken stock
1 cup ground beef, pork, or chicken (can be ground in food processor)
1 cup whole-wheat pasta, uncooked
½ cup frozen peas, thawed
½ cup frozen carrots
½ cup fresh, frozen, or canned corn kernels
2 Tbsp grated Parmesan-Reggiano cheese

DIRECTIONS
In a medium saucepan, heat the chicken stock over medium heat.
Work in the meat. Stir in the pasta and vegetables.

Place the mixture in a 9- by 9- by 2-inch casserole baking dish and sprinkle it
with the cheese. Bake at 350 degrees for 30 minutes.

Let the mixture cool, then cut it into squares according to the size of your dog.
(A Great Dane is going to need a slightly larger square than a Toy Poodle!)

Store the squares in sandwich bags for individual portions.
These freeze well and can keep for up to two months.

Cornelia Cochrane Churchill Guest

and Arthur, Winston, Oscar, Pansy, Nelson, Bear, Lily, Roxy, and Cassidy

Owner/Chef

- Cornelia Guest Events

Old Westbury, New York

The Culinary Canine

When New York businesswoman and philanthropist Cornelia Guest says she grew up with animals, one need look no farther than the walls of her house to know that she means it. From the Richard Stone Reeves portraits of Cornelia as a child on her pony, to the painting that depicts her mother—legendary socialite, equestrienne, and *New York Post* gardening columnist C.Z. Guest—astride her horse, Harlequin, alongside her two children on their steeds, to the near life-size rendering of her father—US Open Polo Championship three-time winner Winston Frederick Churchill Guest—the house is a veritable museum of sporting art. Portraits of ancestors share the walls with portraits of dogs and horses, yet the testament to Cornelia's genuine love of animals is very much alive, well, and trailing behind her as she strolls through the beautiful gardens of her estate. Nine dogs, all rescues, share this abode with the champion horsewoman, who has recently started catering events and marketing her own line of vegan cookies.

"I was the kind of kid who brought home every animal that needed a home, and I haven't strayed very far," laughs the longtime volunteer and advocate for the Humane Society of the United States. Her latest rescue is a three-month-old Chihuahua she dubbed "Oscar" because someone found him in a Los Angeles Dumpster while she was nearby for Elton John's Oscar party. "Can you imagine living your life in a Dumpster?" she says as she shakes her head in astonishment. "My vet told Oscar he had definitely changed his lifestyle!"

After her mother's death from ovarian cancer in 2003, Cornelia became a vegetarian. Several years later, she gave up all animal products, embracing veganism because she "had never felt better, and it was the next logical step." "What's that famous quote—'If slaughterhouses had glass walls, no one would eat meat?'" she asks facetiously. "I really believe that."

One culinary obstacle remained, however: finding a food without any animal ingredients that would satisfy her "serious sweet tooth." Frustrated with what was on the market ("too dense"), she spent years (she started tinkering in 2007) perfecting a cookie recipe that would taste good, hold up, and be consistently replicable. "Depending on the weather, things could happen to the batter," she laughs. Cornelia's cookies made their debut at one of the first events that Cornelia

Guest Events, her event-planning company, catered—Estée Lauder executive John Demsey's birthday party in March 2010. The next month, they were included in the gift bags that were distributed at the Humane Society of New York's benefit, bearing the slogan: "No animals were hurt while making these cookies…I just have a few bruises."

For Thanksgiving 2010, Cornelia Guest Events catered meat- and dairy-free meals, which included her signature cookies. "This is our time of harvest, and everything you can harvest is vegan because it comes from Mother Nature," Cornelia notes. She is currently developing a vegan handbag and accessories line while serving as the brand ambassador for Donna Karan. "I personally don't wear

leather, but her clothes are beautiful, and she's incredibly supportive of women and what women are doing," she says.

A lifelong philanthropist, Cornelia has been the chair of numerous charity events, including the Denim & Diamonds Ball in Palm Beach, Florida, to benefit the United States Equestrian Team and the Equestrian Aid Foundation; Elton John at Radio City, which benefitted the Juilliard School and London's Royal Academy of Music; and the Humane Society's 100th Anniversary Benefit. Never one to simply lend her name, Cornelia truly gets involved with every cause with which she is associated, and none is dearer to her heart than giving an abandoned dog a second chance.

Cornelia's Vegan Yummy Critter Treats

*Chef Cornelia says, "If I didn't tell you these were vegan,
neither you nor your pet would ever know!"*
Dr. Khuly's note: *"These vegan treats are sinful! I didn't use cookie cutters;
I just scored the dough with a pizza cutter to make 1-inch squares that could be
broken apart easily. I left them in the oven overnight for extra crispness."*

INGREDIENTS
1 mashed banana
1 cup whole-wheat flour
⅓ cup honey (more or less, depending on the
consistency of the dough)
1 cup rolled oats

DIRECTIONS
Preheat the oven to 325 degrees.

In a bowl, add the mashed banana to the flour and oats, and mix. Slowly add the
honey until the mixture sticks together.

Roll out the dough to about a ¼-inch thickness. Use your favorite
cookie cutters to cut out the treats. Place them on an ungreased cookie sheet
and paint with honey as a glaze.

Bake 15 to 20 minutes until the treats are browned, and then turn off the oven;
if you leave the treats in there for a bit, they will get extra crunchy.

Serve when cooled. They will be devoured!

Mya Mya (Christine) Gyaw

and Tweety and Buddy

Chef/Co-owner

- Rangoon

Philadelphia,
Pennsylvania

The Culinary Canine

Even when she was living in Burma,* Christine Gyaw and her family cooked for their German Shepherds. "We mixed up a large pot of rice and cooked it until it was like porridge. Then we would mix it with a stock we made from beef bones," the chef and part-owner of Philadelphia's Rangoon restaurant explains. "When they were finished, we gave them the bones to chew." According to Christine, there was no commercial dog food in Burma at the time, and her family preferred to cook for their dogs rather than feed them the family's leftovers. "I think it was better for their digestion," she smiles. Her pets certainly seemed to thrive.

Christine left her country in January 1990, when the government closed the schools, leaving her then-nine-year-old daughter without educational alternatives. Her aunt was already in the United States, and she encouraged Christine to come. Leaving her native land was difficult even though she knew that she was doing the right thing; in addition to the lack of educational opportunities for her daughter, there were virtually no job opportunities for a divorced woman in Burma. She cried during the entire layover in Thailand—until her daughter told her to stop. "She told me not to cry because she would take care of me," she recalls.

Christine, who had studied law in Burma, worked as a shampoo girl in a beauty salon in Philly's Chinatown for three years before the opportunity to open a restaurant fell into her lap. A local restaurant owner was having trouble paying his rent and asked Christine if she wanted to take over his lease. She joined forces with two Burmese women she had met in America ("In Burma, all ladies know how to cook," she laughs), and, in 1993, Rangoon was born. Within three years, they had outgrown their original space and relocated to their current, larger location across the street.

Today, Christine is all smiles. She and her two partners own one of the approximately fifteen Burmese restaurants in the country, and business is booming as more and more Americans discover the unique flavors that borrow

---

*In using "Burma" and "Burmese," we respected Christine's preference for the original name of her homeland instead of the English version "Myanmar" that went into effect in 1989.

influences from both Thai and Indian cuisines. Plus, as she promised, Christine's daughter Mya works alongside her mother in the restaurant while pursuing a degree in business. In 2000, Christine's parents, who were then in their seventies, joined their daughter in Philadelphia, and all of Christine's siblings have likewise emigrated. "I like it here," she admits, "and I love air conditioning—something only rich people have in Burma!"

Christine's family also includes her beloved dogs: Tweety, a Chihuahua/ Yorkshire Terrier mix that was a gift from one of her daughter's previous boyfriends ("When they broke up, she kept the dog," she says); and Buddy, a Pekingese who she adopted from a family who was returning to China. Although Christine works six days a week at the restaurant, manning the front of the house and taking her turn over the stove when needed, her parents dote on her canine pair when she is gone. Although Tweety technically belongs to her daughter Mya and Mya's husband, Michael ("Michael is the only one he listens to," shrugs Christine), Christine cannot bear the thought of splitting up the two dogs. Indeed, both of them, who understand only Burmese, wag their tails expectantly when Michael's name is mentioned.

Christine still cooks for her dogs in this country, only in much smaller portions to match their diminutive statures. And, yes, they both seem very content.

Tutu's Rangoon Chicken

Chef Christine says, "Tutu means 'Tweety' in Burmese!
Just like we did in Burma, I cook for my dogs every day, from scratch.
The ginger in this recipe is good for digestion."
This recipe makes four meals for Christine's dogs,
who weigh 9 and 15 pounds.

INGREDIENTS

½ cup minced chicken breast, cooked
½ teaspoon ground ginger
1 cup hot water
½ cup uncooked rolled oats (such as Quaker)

DIRECTIONS

Boil the chicken and ginger together
in 1 cup of water for 10 minutes.

Add the oats and cook for an additional 2 minutes.

Remove from heat, cool, and serve.

Kerry Heffernan

and Benny

Executive Chef

- South Gate

New York,
New York

The Culinary Canine

An avid outdoorsman, Kerry Heffernan has always been inspired by the natural world. He biked through Europe after he graduated from high school and set up camp—literally—in a tent in southern France. While there, he took a job baking croissants. That experience, combined with various jobs in restaurants while still in school, convinced him to attend the Culinary Institute of America in Hyde Park, New York. Kerry graduated second in his class. A second trip to Europe following culinary-school graduation helped season and refine his palate. When he returned, this time to New York City, it was to put down roots.

Kerry spent time working at esteemed Manhattan restaurants such as Montrachet, Le Régence, and Restaurant Bouley, as well as Mondrian, where he served as sous chef, working with Chef Tom Colicchio of *Top Chef* fame. At One Fifth Avenue, in the position of chef de cuisine, Kerry developed the restaurant's trademark fish menu. He went on to become executive chef of the renowned Polo Restaurant in the Westbury Hotel.

In 1998, Kerry was part of the opening staff of Eleven Madison Park as executive chef, and he later became a partner in the restaurant. It was there that he developed his signature cuisine, which he defines as "seasonal modern American, with a lot of French influence." During Kerry's tenure at Eleven Madison Park, the restaurant won numerous accolades, including *Esquire* magazine's "Best New Restaurant" designation and the James Beard Foundation's Award for Outstanding Service in America.

Kerry's installation as executive chef at South Gate, located on Central Park South, is ideal for this passionate saltwater fly fisherman and snowboarder. While he may not be able to hook any big ones or clear many moguls in New York City, he can look to the park's glorious landscape and draw continuous inspiration for his seasonal cuisine. And then there's the added benefit of an occasional romp with his beloved Labradoodle, Benny, who goes almost everywhere with Kerry.

A 30-pound miniature red Labradoodle from Australian lines, Benny came from a breeder in Washington State and is, according to Kerry, "the perfect urban pet." "He is a lovable friend, has great energy, and seems to have a sixth sense about how to behave around people," he elaborates. "In fact, many of his actions are almost human. He will put his arms around you and actually give you a hug!" Benny loves to go wherever Kerry goes, including fishing on his boat during summer weekends in Sag Harbor. He even has his own life vest, although Kerry says he has not yet been tempted to jump overboard. "When I catch a fish, he barks a little until I get it into the hold, and then he just resumes his position, usually standing up on the edge of the boat, gazing into the water," Kerry explains. "It's when he does this that I sometimes forget he's a dog!"

Bacon Bites

Chef Kerry says, "Who doesn't love bacon? Benny is no exception, and he loves these biscuits, which he gets as special treats—sometimes just for being adorable!"

INGREDIENTS
¼ pound bacon, cut into small, thin strips
2 cups organic whole-wheat flour
2 eggs
1 cup water

DIRECTIONS
Preheat oven to 375 degrees.

Render the bacon in a small saucepot until crisp; remove bits and reserve fat. In a small bowl, combine the bacon bits, flour, and eggs, then add ¼ cup of the water and mix. Add water as needed until the mixture is pliable and moist.

Roll the mixture out to a ¼-inch thickness. Cut out shapes with desired cutter (we use a bone shape) and place the biscuits on a greased baking sheet, about ½ inch apart, making sure that they do not touch.

Bake for 20–25 minutes or until light brown. Let cool. If desired, brush a little reserved bacon fat, warmed, on top of each biscuit for special appeal.

Cool, then store in an airtight container in the refrigerator. These biscuits keep in the refrigerator for about two weeks.

Dog "Broth"

Chef Kerry says, "Benny is approximately 25 pounds, so we give him about ¾–1 cup of this vegetable/meat mix. Sometimes we substitute cooked brown rice for his kibble. Either way, he loves it!" This recipe can be made in much larger batches and then frozen in plastic bags for up to two months.

INGREDIENTS

2 large chicken legs (or breasts, if you prefer) with skin and bone
1 medium carrot, peeled and cut into ½-inch chunks
1 quart water
1 cup peas

DIRECTIONS

Place the chicken in a 3-quart saucepot with the carrot and 1 quart of water.
Bring to a simmer; skim off any fat and foam that accumulates.

Simmer for 4 minutes (1 minute if using breasts), then add
the peas and simmer for 5 more minutes.

Remove from heat and allow the
mixture to cool to room temperature.

Take the chicken out of the mixture. Remove the fat, the skin,
all bones, and all cartilage. Work the chicken into large, nuggetlike
pieces and add these pieces back to the broth.

Add ½ cup warm broth (for best rehydration) to 1 cup dry dog food to moisten
kibble. Mix in the vegetables and meat as appropriate for your dog.

Diane Henderiks

and Daisy and Lilly

**Dietitian/
Personal Chef**

Ocean,
New Jersey

Diane Henderiks hails from the Jersey Shore—the region that fostered Bruce Springsteen and Jon Bon Jovi. In fact, in college, she worked as a bartender at the Stone Pony, the legendary club where "the Boss" got his start! Despite her proximity to the legends of rock and roll, you won't find anyone in the Henderiks house—including the two dogs, Daisy the Great Dane and Lilly the Weimaraner—singing for their supper. Diane, a former all-state field hockey player and aerobic instructor, is all about exercise and eating right, and she has made it her personal mission to raise the bar on good-for-you food. "Since when did healthy cooking become a culinary category of its own?" asks the vivacious, forty-something mother of two facetiously. "Any dish can be healthy—it just takes a little finesse."

Diane, a registered dietitian and personal chef, demonstrates that finesse as a regular on-air contributor for *Good Morning America Health* and as a contributing chef/registered dietitian for *Prevention* magazine. Known as the "Dietitian in the Kitchen," she tours the country, appearing at food and wine festivals. She has been featured in the *New York Times* and on television shows including CBS's *The Early Show* and *CBS News*, NBC's *Today Show*, and FOX's *Good Day New York*, as well as programs on CNN, TLC, BetterTV, and Martha Stewart Radio. She is the founder of Diane M. Henderiks, RD, and Associates, LLC, a nutritional consulting company, and is chef and owner of Diane's Daily Dish, a personal chef and catering service. She also teaches culinary classes and prenatal- and sports-nutrition workshops and conducts supermarket tours.

According to Diane, healthy cooking starts with meticulous planning. Each week, she prepares detailed menus with lists of ingredients for her clients as well as for her family. The goal is to devise dishes made with as little salt, sugar, and fat as possible but about as far from "rabbit food" as you can get. "Goodbye romaine salad with balsamic dressing...Hello baby arugula, papaya, and macadamia salad with pomegranate-lime vinaigrette," she illustrates. "How good does that sound?"

Diane talks about her two "flower girls": "We got Lilly when she was six months old, and she was already named. Since we had a Lilly, we decided to get a Daisy. They are best friends." Daisy is Diane's third Great Dane, and Lilly (a.k.a. "the garbage can") is her second Weimaraner. Daisy has one floppy ear, a result of cartilage not forming correctly, but Diane thinks it gives her character. "We call her 'The Donald' because we think it looks like a comb-over!" she laughs.

"The challenge is to keep Great Danes active, or they are just big couch potatoes," says Diane. Lilly runs with Diane every day while Daisy will venture about 500 feet from the house, plant her feet firmly, and refuse to go another step! And Lilly is so attached to Diane that she waits for her behind any closed door, including the front door when Diane goes out. "She is my shadow everywhere I go—even the bathroom!" Diane admits.

Both dogs have made cameo appearances in some of Diane's television segments, including one on dangerous foods for dogs. Because recipe development is part of her career, concocting tasty dishes for Daisy and Lilly is second nature.

Diane's "Muttloaf"

Chef Diane says, "This tasty meatloaf is a favorite, and Daisy and Lilly lick their plates clean when they eat it!" Diane serves her giant-breed dogs 4 to 5 ounces per meal.

INGREDIENTS
2 pounds ground turkey
½ cup red pepper, finely chopped
½ cup carrots, grated
1 cup brown rice, cooked
¼ cup tomato puree
2 Tbsp chicken broth
2 eggs
½ cup fresh whole-wheat bread crumbs
¼ cup Parmesan cheese, grated

DIRECTIONS
Preheat the oven to 350 degrees.

Combine all ingredients in a large bowl—mixing with your clean hands works best.

On a rimmed baking sheet coated with olive oil, form the mixture into the shape of a bone, about 8 inches long and 1½ inches thick. Bake for about 30 minutes or until there is no pink in the center.

Remove from the oven and let stand for about 5 minutes before slicing.

Cool and serve!

Phyllis Kaplowitz

and Diamond

Executive Chef

- Bakers' Best Catering

Boston, Massachusetts

The Culinary Canine

Phyllis Kaplowitz, who graduated from Northeastern University with a degree in political science, wanted to be a journalist, but when job opportunities were scarce, she took a part-time position at the historic Jacob Wirth Restaurant in Boston's theater district. "I started out as a waitress and moved to bartender, then line cook, and eventually general manager," she laughs. In fact, the owners of the restaurant, the Fitzgerald family, put her through Johnson & Wales University's prestigious culinary academy on the school's Providence, Rhode Island, campus, about 50 miles outside Boston. "It was a pretty tough schedule," Phyllis admits. "I would go to school until two in the afternoon and then go to work. But the difference was that I really wanted to be there."

Phyllis graduated at the top of her class in 1999, having mastered a broad array of cooking and executive-management skills, which put her in good stead when Jacob Wirth's underwent a massive renovation. The 140-year-old restaurant was named "Best Neighborhood Restaurant" by *Boston Magazine* in 2003 and was listed as one of the top ten places to eat in Boston on Food TV's website while Phyllis was executive chef. Its clam chowder remains legendary.

Phyllis joined Bakers' Best Catering in 2006. She was attracted to the high-end caterer because she loves putting on events. "I always thought that it was one of my best talents," she smiles. Certainly such clients as the Boston Celtics, the Boston Bruins, New England Patriots owner Robert Kraft, and Boston's Mayor Thomas Menino agree with that assessment! Phyllis is also a familiar figure on both the regional and national food-media circuit, having appeared on *Phantom Gourmet*, *TV Diner*, the radio show *The Olives Table* with Todd English, and Food Network's *Chopped* in May 2011.

While she may have severed her professional ties to Jacob Wirth's, Phyllis remains extremely friendly with her former employers, Robin and Kevin Fitzgerald, who own the restaurant. In fact, it was the Fitzgeralds—"huge animal lovers," according to Phyllis—who had originally rescued Diamond. "I think Robin's penchant for rescuing animals started slowly," Phyllis explains. "She would take her dog to the vet and learn of an animal in need, so she would bring it home." Eventually, the Fitzgeralds' farm (which they named "So What's One

More?") was, according to Phyllis, home to "about twenty dogs, multiple cats, and at least a dozen horses." Robin would find homes for some, but many would stay forever. "She feels fortunate to be in a position to be able to provide care for many animals that might not get it otherwise," says Phyllis.

Diamond caught Phyllis's eye when Robin brought the American Bulldog to work one day when she was about four months old. "It was love at first sight," Phyllis admits. "She looked like a marshmallow." The attraction was not only mutual but also fortuitous, because the Fitzgeralds had already determined that Diamond would be better in an environment with fewer dogs. That attribute has not changed ("We call her 'the diva,'" admits Phyllis), but Diamond has found a forever home, with Phyllis and her husband as her adoring subjects.

"Diamond commands attention, and she gets it," admits Phyllis. "She likes people more than dogs, and she is not above reprimanding us for leaving her in the care of a dog sitter when we go out of town. When we come home, she is so excited to see us, but then she remembers that we left her, so she does not give us

any attention for a day or so."

When Diamond developed a growth on top of her ear that turned out to be a mast-cell tumor, Phyllis went into overdrive, researching nutritional information about cancer. While Diamond's surgery in 2007 was extremely successful, Phyllis remains committed to keeping more omega-3 oils in Diamond's diet. "So far, so good," she smiles. "I try to do whatever I can to prolong her life. I've always had a strong love for animals, but seeing Robin and Kevin's devotion to their animals has made me even more responsible toward mine."

Diamond's Favorite Salmon Cakes with Yogurt Tartar Sauce

Chef Phyllis says, "Two years ago, Diamond was diagnosed with a mast-cell tumor. I was anguished, thinking that I might have caused this through her lifestyle or diet. After doing extensive research, I found a lot of information and studies on the benefits of salmon and omega-3 fish oil in the diets of domesticated canines. Salmon gives dogs energy, helps their hearts, and improves their coats. If the salmon cakes are too labor-intensive, just add a few tablespoons of canned salmon to your dog's diet."

INGREDIENTS

For yogurt tartar sauce:
¼ cup plain low-fat or fat-free yogurt
½ tsp dried parsley

For salmon cakes:
1 14.5-ounce can of wild Alaskan salmon or 1
   pound fresh wild salmon
2 egg whites
¼ cup low-fat or fat-free yogurt
½ cup sugar-free oatmeal or sugar-free crisp rice
   cereal, ground
2 tsp dried parsley
½ cup raw carrot, shredded

DIRECTIONS

Mix together the yogurt and dried parsley. Cover and refrigerate the sauce until the salmon cakes are cool.

Preheat the oven to 375 degrees. If you are using fresh salmon, bake it on a cookie sheet for 20 minutes. If using canned salmon, drain the liquid.

In a medium bowl, mix together the salmon, egg whites, shredded carrots, and yogurt. In a separate bowl, mix together the oatmeal or rice cereal with the dried parsley.

Using a large spoon or rounded scooper, scoop out one ball of the salmon mixture and lightly flatten it into a patty. Dredge or thoroughly coat the patty in the cereal/parsley mixture. Place the patty on a cookie sheet, either lightly greased or lined with parchment paper. Repeat until you've used all of the salmon mixture to form patties.

Bake for 12 minutes or until lightly browned, then flip the cakes and bake for an additional 12 minutes or until lightly browned. Cool the cakes completely on a wire rack before serving with the yogurt tartar sauce.

This recipe makes eight to ten cakes. Feed one or two cakes per meal, depending on your dog's size. You can supplement with brown rice or even dog kibble if you want; again, portions will vary depending on the size of your dog.

Nick Lacasse

and Sophie

Executive Chef

- The Drawing Room

  Chicago, Illinois

The Culinary Canine

Nick Lacasse grew up in Williston, Vermont, where his grandparents owned a dairy farm. "I was milking cows by the age of four," the chef laughs. "Being exposed to farming at such a young age definitely influenced my cooking style, which relies heavily on seasonal ingredients from local purveyors." And while Nick left the Green Mountain State at the age of eighteen for Portland, Oregon, where he got his first experience in the food industry, he made several return trips over the years to perfect his craft. In fact, his prowess at Etta's Seafood in Seattle earned him a scholarship to the New England Culinary Institute, located in Vermont's capital city of Montpelier.

Upon graduation, Nick moved to Portland, Maine, where he worked at Hugo's and "learned so much about food." He decided to "try out" Chicago in late 2002 and landed a job at Charlie Trotter's. He then helped open Trotter's To Go, the restaurant's catering operation. "It was a good experience, but it wasn't a restaurant," Nick admits. Which is why, in 2004, he jumped at the opportunity to work at Spring restaurant for legendary Chicago chef Sean McClain, who would go on to win the James Beard Award for Best Chef: Midwest in 2006. Nick left McClain on good terms in late 2005, opened a small catering venture, and earned enough money to backpack through Central America for six months. When he returned to Chicago in 2006, he helped McClain open Green Zebra, a mostly vegetarian establishment, followed by Custom House, with a varied menu of meat, seafood, and vegetable dishes.

McClain is the consulting chef at The Drawing Room, which bills itself as a "culinary cocktail lounge." While the drinks are mixed tableside, the food is prepared in the kitchen under the direction of Nick, who hired and trained his staff. "It has been an education, but this is my baby," he says. Known for his emphasis on seasonality as well as unconventional flavor combinations, Nick has earned stellar reviews in *Food & Wine*, *Gourmet*, the *Chicago Sun-Times*, and the *Chicago Tribune* as well as nearly all of Chicago's gourmet- and food-focused websites and blogs. He takes the best from the best and still manages to add his own signature to the classics. A Greek salad, for example, includes grilled octopus, goat's feta, oil-cured olives, and shaved cucumbers. The fish in the fish and chips are cod "beignets" and the "burger" is actually a slice of delicate short rib.

Sophie, a rescue from a local shelter, came into Nick's life during his first year at The Drawing Room. Nick and his then-girlfriend adopted her together because they fell in love with her on the spot. Sadly, the girlfriend left, but Sophie stayed, which turned out to be just the antidote for a broken heart. "Having to walk Sophie got me up and out, so no moping. The late-night walks after I come home from the restaurant continue to be very relaxing for me," he says. "It's a good way to defuse after the intensity of the kitchen."

There was a time, however, especially during hot weather, when Sophie was prone to sitting down and refusing to budge. Nick was so concerned that he took

her to the vet, who reported that Sophie was fine. The vet speculated that she might have been hot or tired. Now, if and when Sophie takes a break, Nick waits patiently for her to get up.

Their favorite activities include football in the backyard with a Nerf football and vigorous games of "snappy," in which Nick snaps a wool winter scarf and Sophie tries to catch it in mid-air in her mouth. "She could do that for hours," he smiles.

Nick was curious enough about Sophie's heredity to get her DNA analyzed. What he discovered is that his mixed breed is predominantly German Shorthaired Pointer with a little Rottweiler, some Collie, and a drop of Australian Cattle Dog. "Whatever she is, she's great!" he laughs.

Sophie's Green Bean Casserole with Sweet Potato, Thyme, Oats, and Bone Marrow

Chef Nick says, "My veterinarian suggested that I add some vegetables to Sophie's diet, so I developed this recipe for her. Sophie loves her veggies!"

INGREDIENTS

4 pieces of 3-inch crosscut marrow bones
Salt
1 pound fresh green beans, cut into 1-inch pieces
1 medium sweet potato or yam, peeled and
  chopped
1 cup rolled oats
Olive oil
Honey
Sprigs of thyme

DIRECTIONS

Blanch the marrow bones by placing them in a pot, covering them with cold water, and bringing to a simmer. Remove from heat. Place the pot in the sink and run cold water over the bones until cooled. With your thumb, push out the marrow from the center of the bones and dice small. Set aside.

Put a slightly salted pot of water on high heat and preheat the oven to 350 degrees. Add green beans and simmer for about 5 minutes until very soft (or slightly less if your pooch likes a little more crunch). Set aside.

Place the sweet potato or yam pieces in the same water and simmer until tender but not mushy.

Place the pieces on a rack to air-dry for about 10 minutes. When dried, put the pieces on a baking sheet, sprinkle with oats, and drizzle with a little bit of honey, olive oil, and some thyme sprigs. Roast for about 25 minutes until the potato or yam starts to caramelize around the edges. Remove the thyme sprigs and set them aside.

To serve, place a couple spoonfuls of the oat/ sweet potato (or yam) mixture on a plate and top with green beans and diced marrow. To garnish, pinch thyme leaves from the sprigs; they will be dried and fall from stems easily.

This is enough for two to four meals, depending on the size and appetite of your dog.

Matthew Levin

and Sadie and Arthur

Chef/Part Owner

- Adsum

Philadelphia,
Pennsylvania

It's not easy to succeed a legend. That's one of the reasons Chef Matthew Levin turned down the opportunity to become executive chef at Philadelphia's famed Lacroix the first time that the job became available. Sure enough, the first chef who followed the revered Chef Jean-Marie Lacroix in his namesake restaurant lasted only a few months. The second time that the job was offered to him, however, Matt jumped at the chance. From the time he joined the famous Lacroix kitchen in late 2006 until he left in 2009, Matt proved that good things are worth waiting for. The *Philadelphia Inquirer* food critic Craig LaBan called his cuisine "Philly's most sophisticated contemporary cooking," awarding Lacroix a rare and elite four-bell status.

Matthew Levin is used to attracting attention for his culinary creativity. Since his graduation from the prestigious Culinary Institute of America in Hyde Park, New York, he has made it his practice to learn from the finest chefs in his native Philadelphia area, including Georges Perrier of Le Bec-Fin and the now-shuttered Brasserie Perrier and Craig Shelton, who was named Best Chef: Mid Atlantic by the James Beard Foundation in 2000 while at the Ryland Inn in Whitehouse, New Jersey. Matt worked his way up to executive chef at Moonlight Restaurant in New Hope, Pennsylvania, where he garnered national attention. *Bon Appétit* reported that his "culinary creations now share the spotlight with art, thanks to 'Moonlight,'" while *American Way* magazine wrote that Moonlight was a "hot spot worth the hike."

Matt's cooking style is a unique blend of Spanish, Portuguese, Thai, Japanese, and American flavors infused with his own custom-made spices, which he says that he prepares with "the latest techniques and a little bit of molecular gastronomy." He was recently featured on the Food Network's series of shows about molecular food and is particularly intrigued by the ways that techniques transform ingredients. At heart, Matt is an adventurer. He is not afraid to try new combinations of foods or spices to add a hint of surprise to his dishes.

His latest venture is Adsum, a "neighborhood bistro" in Philadelphia's Queen Village section and adjacent to its famed Fabric Row. The area reminds Matt of his father, who was in the fabric business. One of Matt's partners in this venture is former Eagles tackle and New Jersey congressman Jon Runyan. "This is a small, down-and-dirty neighborhood bistro," Matt says. "Before, I always cooked the food that the press and *Food Arts* magazine wanted me to cook. I want to make food that people can eat—finger-lickin' good fried chicken. Just grub. Eat."

Matt, who grew up with Collies, knew that he wanted his children, Sammy and Noah, to grow up with big dogs. "These guys are all dog," he says fondly of his two Weimaraners, Sadie and Arthur. "You can really play and wrestle with them." The family fell in love with the breed when they spied a Weimaraner puppy "spread out on all fours because he had lost his balance" while on a family vacation. "This puppy was so adorable in that gangly all-legs stage that I knew we had found the right [breed] for us," recalls Matt. Although the boys came home from vacation with only hermit crabs, Arthur joined the family a few months later. Sadie followed about three years later to keep Arthur company.

After a colleague at Lacroix lost his cat because of pet food involved in the 2007 recall, Matt decided to cook for his own dogs. "I didn't want to take any chances," he said. "These guys are part of my family." Sadie and Arthur love nothing more than to sit in the leather chair by the window and watch the world go by, especially if that world involves squirrels, rabbits, or birds. "They are hunting dogs, after all," smiles Matt.

Matt takes his role as dog chef very seriously, and Sadie and Arthur eat extremely well. "They're fat dogs in skinny dogs' bodies," he says with a trace of envy. "They eat a lot, but they burn it all off."

Note: *Since our photo shoot, Matt lost Arthur to a rare bacterial lung infection that did not respond to treatment. He has since adopted Clyde, another Weimaraner; and Señor Howie Tartuffo, a Boston Terrier.*

Arthur's Lamb Fricassee

Chef Matt says, "I developed this recipe for my late dog, Arthur, but Sadie, Clyde, and Howie love it as well. This recipe makes six servings for large dogs; I give Howie half the amount I give to Sadie and Clyde. Right before I serve this to my dogs, I add a tablespoon each of flax seeds and bone meal. If you add the flax seeds and bone meal too early, the mixture can spoil quickly."

INGREDIENTS

3 cups cooked brown rice

2 pounds lean ground lamb (can substitute ground chicken, beef, or turkey)

1 bag frozen peas

6 carrots, peeled and diced

4 Yukon Gold potatoes, blanched and diced

2 red apples, cored, with seeds removed, and diced

4 Tbsp safflower oil

5 cups chicken stock

6 Tbsp flax seeds, divided

1 Tbsp bee pollen, finely ground

6 Tbsp bone meal, divided

Sea salt to taste

(yes, taste your dog's food)

DIRECTIONS

In a heavy-bottomed sauce pot, add the oil and heat it until it smokes. Add the lamb (or whatever meat you are using) and brown it well. Add the potatoes to the pot and continue cooking for 5 minutes. Add the apples, chicken stock, and peas to the pot. Bring to a boil and then reduce to a simmer; cook for 10 minutes. Season with sea salt to taste.

Remove the mixture from the heat and add the carrots. (I add them at the end because I've found that my dogs like the crunch that they add.)

Let the mixture cool, then mix in the brown rice and bee pollen. The food can be stored in the refrigerator in a covered container for two days or frozen for up to two months.

Sadie & Clyde's Cookies

Chef Matt says, "These cookies don't spread because of the lack of fat, so it's best to press them down before baking. My dogs love these cookies! They are a bit dry (although quite good) for humans to eat, so it's best to leave them for the pups."

INGREDIENTS

3 cups whole-wheat flour
1 cup rolled oats
1 cup Grape Nuts cereal
1 cup natural peanut butter
1 cup vegetable oil
2 Tbsp baking powder
1 cup smoked honey (regular honey will do)
1 cup water
1 beef bouillon cube

DIRECTIONS

Preheat oven to 325 degrees.

Combine all of the ingredients in a mixing bowl until well combined.

Drop the mixture by teaspoons onto a nonstick cookie sheet and press each spoonful with your palm or the bottom of a glass to flatten.

Bake for approximately 15–20 minutes or until browned. Let cool before serving.

These cookies store well in a tightly covered container. They will last for about two weeks, but will probably be devoured long before then.

Anita Lo
and Mochi and Adzuki

Chef/Owner

- Annisa

New York,
New York

At one point in her youth, Anita Lo wanted to be a doctor like her mother. At another, she harbored what she now calls "pipe dreams" of being a concert pianist. As a French major at Columbia University, she thought that she might work at the United Nations. All of that changed when she lived in Paris during her junior year in college and took a cooking course. "I was hooked," she admits. Upon graduation, she took at job at the then-year-old French restaurant Bouley in lower Manhattan, where she rationalized that she could, at the very least, keep up with her French. One year later, she returned to Paris and enrolled at the famed Ritz Escoffier cooking school, from which she graduated first in her class.

After graduation, Anita secured several internships in Paris under such noted chefs as Michel Rostang and Guy Savoy. Returning to New York, she worked her way through all of the kitchen stations at Chanterelle; took a job as chef at Can, a French-Vietnamese restaurant in SoHo; and eventually settled at the New York incarnation of Maxim's, owned by the late fashion designer Pierre Cardin. After Maxim's, she moved to Mirezi, where she began earning rave reviews, including a glowing one from Ruth Reichl in the *New York Times*. She has appeared on programs on CNN, the Food Network, CBS, and NBC, including the *Martha Stewart Show*.

After two years at Mirezi, Anita and her business partner at the time, Jennifer Scism, spent the better part of a year traveling the globe in search of the ultimate meal. They returned to Manhattan's Greenwich Village in 2000 and opened Annisa, one of only two female-owned restaurants to earn a coveted star in the 2007 New York edition of the *Michelin Guide*. Almost immediately, the forty-five-seat date-night place, which one reviewer called "quietly ambitious, elegant without being fussy," became known for its inventive take on contemporary American food with subtle Asian influences and, according to the *New York Times*, "informed by classical French technique."

Food & Wine magazine chose Anita as one of its Best New Chefs in 2001. Anita bested Mario Batali in "Battle: Mushrooms" on Food Network's *Iron Chef* in 2005, and she also competed in the first season of *Top Chef Masters* in 2007. In short, she became known as one of the finest chefs in the world. And then, in July 2007—two weeks before the first episode of *Top Chef Masters* was scheduled to air—

an electrical fire broke out in the kitchen of Annisa and destroyed the restaurant. "It could have taken three months to rebuild, but instead it took nine," Anita acknowledges. Reopen it did, however, in April 2010, and the praise has been ongoing. "The layout is the same," says Anita, "but we have nicer chairs and darker woods. It feels renewed." Anita's food, notes one reviewer, is "as good as any she has made in her career."

While rebuilding Annisa, Anita worked on her cookbook, *Cooking without Borders*, which she says is about her multicultural cuisine and how to put it together. Also an avid fisher and gardener, she relishes spending time at her retreat on Long Island, as do her constant companions, Shih Tzus Mochi and Adzuki. "I always wanted a dog as a kid, but I was allergic," says Anita. "I remember getting fixated on a Samoyed and my mom giving me a plush version that just wasn't going to cut it."

Anita's Shih Tzus were the choice of her girlfriend at the time. Mochi, who came first ("an expensive rescue," jokes Anita), was chosen because she was

small and didn't shed. Alas, Anita still endured two months of hives (and antihistamines) until, one day, the allergies disappeared. Eventually, so did the girlfriend—without the dogs. By then, there were two, because Anita wanted a dog of her own. She also thought that Mochi needed company because he, too, was developing skin problems. "He stopped itching as soon as we got

Adzuki, which was about a year later," she says.

The pair is pretty much inseparable and devoted to Anita. Mochi is the more outgoing; Adzuki is a bit more reserved when it comes to strangers and is frightened of loud noises, including the clicking of the camera shutter. Both hang out in the front window of the restaurant during the day ("I trained in France, where dogs are a fixture in restaurants," says Anita) and often ride around their Greenwich Village neighborhood in the basket of Anita's bike. Nothing makes them happier than when Anita gets their leashes and takes them on walks. When the restaurant is open, they do go home, where they fall asleep—dreaming of leftovers, no doubt.

Roasted Filet of Bluefish with Roasted Yams, Peas, and Bacon

Chef Anita says, "Because Mochi has allergies, fish and yams are staples in her diet. You can substitute another oily fish, such as salmon, for bluefish in this recipe." This recipe makes four servings for a Shih Tzu-sized dog.

Dr. Khuly's note: "This recipe makes a delightful 'bluefish hash.' Served with eggs, stewed tomatoes, and Chef Kerry Heffernan's Bacon Bites, you'd have quite a canine brunch!"

INGREDIENTS
1 large yam
1 Tbsp oil
2 slices bacon
½ pound bluefish filets, skin off, bloodlines removed
½ cup (cooked) frozen peas, defrosted

DIRECTIONS
Preheat the oven to 375 degrees.

Cut the yam in half lengthwise and coat it with the oil. Place it in a baking dish, cut-side down, and roast until soft—about 20 minutes, depending on the thickness.

About 5 minutes before the yam is done, place the bacon strips in the baking dish next to the yam and top the yam and bacon with the bluefish filets. Roast for about 5 minutes or until cooked through.

Remove the skins from the yams and chop the yams. Place all roasted ingredients in a bowl with the peas and lightly mix them together.

Cool and serve.

Tanya Nunes

and Mz. Maggie

Owner

- Chef Tanya, Inc.

  Daly City, California

The Culinary Canine

What's a nice girl from a Portuguese Catholic family doing catering strictly kosher affairs in the San Francisco Bay area? "Changing the face of kosher cooking!" laughs Tanya Nunes, owner of Chef Tanya. "Kosher food doesn't have to be flavorless, overcooked, and dry. It's all about fresh ingredients and making everything from scratch. My motto is: good food that happens to be kosher."

Nunes, a fifth-generation Californian (on both sides of the family), grew up surrounded by good food. Her paternal grandparents ran a butcher shop for decades, and she grew up eating the finest and freshest food available, including fruits and vegetables from her own backyard. She moved to the East Coast in 1993 to attend college and took a job as a nanny for an Orthodox Jewish family in Philadelphia to help pay the bills. She had a "crash course" in Judaism, taught by the grandfather, a rabbi, who instructed her on how to keep kosher. Her duties included cooking for the family on Shabbat, a task that she took very seriously. "Growing up in Northern California with so many ethnic influences, I was taking the kosher thing to a level they hadn't really seen," Tanya laughs. "I'd do Mexican dairy, for example. The family ended up buying better dairy dishes because I made so many nice dairy meals." (Kosher cooking separates meat and dairy, which are served on different sets of dishes.)

The meals were so good that the matriarch of the family told Tanya that she should drop out of college, enroll in Philadelphia's Restaurant School, and become a famous chef—which is exactly what she did. Her education included an apprenticeship with Georges Perrier, owner of the famed Le Bec-Fin, Philadelphia's first five-star restaurant. Upon graduating in 1995, Tanya moved back to California to take care of her ailing grandmother, and she "bounced around" to different jobs. In 1998, while working for Rent-A-Chef, she was hired by the vice president of Oracle, thus beginning a long stint of cooking for the Silicon Valley elite. In 2002, Tanya did a consulting job in Japan for the United States Navy aboard the U.S.S. Blue Ridge in Tokyo Bay.

A few years later, the Culinary Institute of California asked Tanya to cater a kosher event. "I know how to do that!" was her response, and from then on, mostly through word of mouth, her kosher catering business, as she puts it, "took off."

Tanya, who converted to Judaism in 2009, loves being part of people's celebrations: "I like bringing new and interesting things to events, and I want to be the new face of kosher cooking. In this day of mass-produced food, it is good to know where your food comes from. When there is a kashrut seal on the package, you know that someone is paying attention and monitoring the system."

Tanya even cooks kosher food for her beloved black Lab/Golden Retriever-mix rescue dog, Mz. Maggie, who has a food allergy to corn and wheat. "When I walked into the Silicon Valley Humane Society, Mz. Maggie was the first dog I saw," she recalls. "After the adoption counselor brought her to me for us to meet, Mz. Maggie put her paw on my leg and let her tongue fall to the side of her mouth like, 'I love you, take me home.' It was love at first sight." Mz. Maggie, in fact, went on to become the "poster dog" for the Silicon Valley Humane Society! "She is the most loving and kind dog," Tanya says. "When we walk down the street, people routinely say, 'Look at that happy dog.' She is super mellow, loves people and kids, emits love, and has never attended a party that she did not like!"

Over time, Tanya began to notice that Mz. Maggie was developing dry, itchy, skin lesions and losing clumps of fur. It was only when Tanya developed the Kosher for Passover recipe with quinoa about three years ago and fed it to Mz. Maggie that she suspected a corn and wheat allergy. "When she ate the Passover food, she had no skin issues," Tanya remarks. Since going gluten-free, Mz. Maggie, according to Tanya, has "stopped itching and has maintained a svelte 65-pound physique. She even has a patch of gray hair under her chin that has been slowly turning back to black!"

Quinoa, which is a high-protein, gluten-free grain, is a great addition to everyone's diets—even those who don't keep kosher for Passover. "This is an all-year-long recipe that I do not have to modify for Passover," notes Tanya.

Kosher for Passover Dog Food

Chef Tanya says, "During Passover, observant Jews can't own anything that contains chometz (wheat, barley, corn, rice, legumes). This recipe for your pooch is kosher for Passover and is so delicious that your dog will want Pesach to last the whole year! The quinoa is very rich in protein, and the flax makes dogs' coats look shiny." If you do not follow the dietary laws, you do not have to use kosher meat to make this recipe. All of the other ingredients are considered kosher.

INGREDIENTS
4 cups water
2 cups quinoa
¼ cup ground flaxseed meal
½ cup shredded carrots
1 pound raw ground meat from a kosher butcher—
beef, chicken, turkey, and lamb are all acceptable

DIRECTIONS
Cook the quinoa by bringing the 4 cups of water and quinoa to a boil in a covered pot. Let the quinoa boil on high for 3 minutes. Turn off the heat and let the quinoa steam.

When the quinoa is cool enough to handle, add the flaxseed meal, carrot, and meat. Combine by hand until evenly mixed.

Feed your dog according to his or her weight and activity level, generally about ⅓ cup of food for every 15 pounds.

You can store this food in a covered container in the refrigerator for up to three days. It is best not to freeze this recipe, although the meat can be frozen separately and then defrosted before combining with the other ingredients.

Marc Penvenne

and Rex

Chef/Owner

- Méli-Mélo
Crêperie

Greenwich,
Connecticut

The Culinary Canine

Since 1993, there has been a line outside the door of Chef Marc Penvenne's establishment, Méli-Mélo Crêperie, on Greenwich Avenue. It starts at ten o'clock in the morning, when he opens the doors, and continues until ten o'clock at night, when he calls it a day. Clearly, the mixture of fresh, all-natural ingredients, prepared to the highest standards and combined with affordable prices and casual atmosphere, is anything but "hodgepodge," the literal translation of the establishment's name. "The French have a gene for food," laughs Marc, who grew up in the Brittany region of France. "There is no great secret to my recipes. I go to the market two or three times a week to get the freshest produce. Freshness makes all the difference."

Penvenne came to Greenwich via St. Barths, where his two children were born and where he contemplated opening a crêperie. "But to be on St. Barths twelve months a year would be boring," says the vibrant Frenchman, who rarely sits still. When it came time for the children to go to school, he and his wife, Evelyn, relocated to Greenwich, where he opened Méli-Mélo in 1993. In 2006, he expanded for the first time, opening an additional catering kitchen a few doors down. In 2010, he took over the space next door, doubling the size of the restaurant's seating area.

Celebrated by both *Zagat* (which awarded Méli-Mélo twenty-five out of thirty points for food in its 2010/2011 guide) and the *New York Times* (who called it a "little space with quite a mélange" that can "transform a meal on the run from a necessity to a pleasure"), Marc has become a well-known and well-loved fixture in the community. In fact, he can often be spotted on the main drag, Greenwich Avenue, being taken for a walk by his family's spirited and charismatic Yorkshire Terrier, Rex. "When my wife, Evelyn, and I met for the first time, a long time ago in France, she had a Yorkshire Terrier," he says. "I fell in love with her and her dog!"

Everyone falls in love with Rex, who technically belonged to the couple's daughter until she moved to Manhattan after college. No matter—Rex quickly became the object of Evelyn and Marc's adoration and affection, and they have special fun when they open their swimming pool for the summer. "We really enjoy summertime with Rex," Marc says. "He loves running and diving into the pool. In fact, we do it together! Rex is a great swimmer and loves the water."

He also is fiercely protective of all members of the family. "Rex is very brave and courageous," explains Marc. "Anyone who comes to the house needs to be warned. We have a sign at the front door in French that reads *Chien Bizarre* [bizarre dog]." Rex's huge personality is pretty amazing for a little guy who was sick with pancreatitis for almost a year as a puppy. The vet prescribed a very strict diet, with no processed food. Marc is meticulous about measuring out the exact proportions of meat, carbohydrates, fiber, and vitamins and varying the ingredients in Rex's food to keep him happy and healthy.

"In many ways, Rex and I are very similar," remarks Marc. "We both handle situations in the same way. When Rex is in a bad mood, no one can approach him, just like me. I know when to leave him alone."

Rex's Dog Food

Chef Marc says, "Rex developed pancreatitis at a young age. I sought help from our veterinarian, who put me in contact with a veterinary dietician. We worked together to develop Rex's recipe, and he has been happy and healthy since."

INGREDIENTS

Protein source:
Organic chicken, poached, with no skin
Loin of rabbit, sautéed, with no fat and no skin
Loin of lean meat such as ostrich or buffalo, sautéed, with no fat
(Occasionally) fresh turkey, sautéed, with no fat
White and lean fish (no salmon or tuna)

Carbohydrate source (cooked in water):
White rice
Pasta
Corn
Peas
Barley
Oatmeal

Fiber source:
Cooked vegetables, such as green beans, broccoli, baby spinach, carrots, sweet potatoes, or squash
As a treat, raw carrot, English cucumber (no seeds), or the crunchy part of lettuce

DIRECTIONS

Choose one ingredient from each category—protein, carbohydrate, and fiber—along with vitamins as recommended by your veterinarian. Combine the chosen ingredients in a food processor or blender in the following proportions:
Protein: 75 grams
Carbohydrate: 128 grams
Fiber: 35 grams
Vitamins: 6.5 grams

One ounce equals 28 grams, but because the conversion results in uneven amounts (meat would be 2.68 ounces for example), you are better off using the metric measurements to ensure the proper proportion.

Note: This recipe was developed specifically for Rex's needs; this recipe makes two meals a day for Rex. To adapt it to your dog's needs, you have to adjust not only the weight of the food according to your dog's weight but also the ratio of the ingredients to each other. All of this is possible, but you should consult with your own veterinarian for specific instructions.

Melissa Perello

and Dingo

Executive Chef

- Frances

San Francisco,
California

Melissa Perello is taking the culinary world by storm. In September 2010, her restaurant, Frances, was recognized by *Bon Appétit* magazine as one of the top ten restaurants in the country, a significant laurel to add to her growing collection, which includes recognition as one of *Food & Wine*'s "Best New Chefs" in 2004 as well as several James Beard nominations. All of this while still in her thirties!

Melissa grew up on the East Coast in Nutley, New Jersey, and she knew that she wanted to go to culinary school before she entered high school. She was an ardent devotee of cooking shows on television (in those days, this meant strictly PBS shows featuring chefs such as Julia Child, Nathalie Dupree, and Graham Greene, the "Galloping Gourmet"); one day, Melissa's mother came home to find her twelve-year-old daughter deboning a leg of lamb! Melissa got her first professional job when her family moved to Houston during her high-school years. She got a position in the kitchen of the local country club, where she worked "forty hours and pretty much didn't do much else."

While attending the Culinary Institute of America in Hyde Park, New York, Melissa vacationed in San Francisco, where she dined at Aqua. A fortuitous conversation (and an invite into the kitchen) with then-chef de cuisine, Mark LoRusso, led first to an externship with executive chef, Michael Mina, and then, following graduation, a full-time position. After two years at Aqua, Melissa transferred to its nearby sister restaurant, Charles Nob Hill, where she worked with Chef Ron Siegel. When Siegel left in 2001, Melissa took over his role and began to put together a long string of successes. "I have been very fortunate," she acknowledges. "Things just took off right away."

And how! After a stint as executive chef at the renowned Fifth Floor that resulted in the restaurant's earning a Michelin star in 2006, Melissa ventured out on her own to open, in December 2009, a small (thirty-seven seats plus ten at the bar) neighborhood place, which she remodeled with her father and named after her grandmother—Frances. The limited menu changes daily and features entrées that are priced moderately (even for San Francisco) and showcase local produce and ingredients. The atmosphere is casual, the wait for a reservation is over three months, and the line for those without one begins to form at 4:45 in

the afternoon. Frances is yet another triumph for the chef, who one critic says "has the all-too-rare ability to transcend the mechanics of cooking to express a point of view, to change the way we taste and think."

Melissa adopted Dingo, a "certified mutt," from Berkeley's Milo Foundation, one of the sponsors of an adoption fair that she attended. "I wasn't actually looking for a dog, but I am a big fan of this organization. When I saw Dingo, however, it was love at first sight! I had to take him home that day," she says unabashedly. "He came with a tag that said he had been adopted twice before, but something between us just clicked. He is super-cute and docile, and he warmed up to me really quickly. He essentially chose me and has been my buddy ever since."

Their camaraderie has included a camping trip to Olallie Lake in Oregon—"just the snout and me," as Melissa puts it. "We went swimming. I took him on a paddle boat, and we went hiking," she continues. "It was serene, relaxing, and just an awesome trip."

As for his name, well, according to Melissa, a friend did some research, and it seems as if her "certifiable mutt" is actually an American Dingo, also known as a Carolina Dog. Regardless of his pedigree or lack thereof, Dingo has ended up being nothing less than the "perfect dog." "He's active when I am, and when I want to sleep in, he's more than happy to do so," Melissa notes. "He's mellow, cool, and so cute!"

Dingo was getting a little thick around the middle, so Melissa has taken to restricting his food, although she does admit that he gets his fair share of "good meat scraps from the restaurant." While Dingo may be, as Melissa suggests, "very spoiled," there is also no doubt that he is very much loved.

Doggy Dinners

Chef Melissa says, "Dingo really loves lamb, and this recipe is easy to make and healthy. The experience of cooking for him is an activity we can share—I cook, and he sniffs the aromas appreciatively! I like to make this dish overnight in a 6-quart Dutch oven."

INGREDIENTS

1 small bone-in lamb shoulder, approximately 4–5 pounds (you can also use cubed lamb chuck or even shanks for an extra-special treat, or you can substitute a small chicken)
1½ cups farro, spelt, or barley
2 large carrots, peeled, washed, and chopped into 1-inch pieces
2 ribs celery, washed and chopped into 1-inch pieces
½ bunch hearty kale, such as Lacinato or Dinosaur kale, washed and chopped into 1-inch pieces
Small bundle of herbs (such as thyme or rosemary)
3½ cups sweet peas, steamed
½ cup extra virgin olive oil
3¾ cups leftover chicken broth
Water

DIRECTIONS

Preheat the oven to 280 degrees. Place the lamb and all other ingredients in a Dutch oven with enough water to cover. Cover everything with a sheet of parchment paper and the lid.

Put the pot in the oven. Remove after 6 to 8 hours. Gently pull the lamb from the pot to remove the bones and shred the meat. Return the meat to the pot and incorporate with the rest of the ingredients.

This recipe makes at least four doggy meals for a dog of Dingo's size, which is about 90 pounds. The food can be stored in the refrigerator in a covered container for three to four days.

Georges Perrier

and Isabelle

Chef/Proprietor

- Le Bec-Fin

Philadelphia,
Pennsylvania

- Georges'

Wayne,
Pennsylvania

Oh, to be Isabelle and dine exclusively on la cuisine Perrier! *C'est la vie!* For all of her life, the Bichon Frise has dined on recipes created and prepared for her by her doting owner, Georges Perrier, one of the world's most renowned chefs. Once a month, the member of the French National Order of Merit (the second-highest distinction accorded by France to civilians; Perrier has been awarded Knight status) prepares Isabelle's food at one of his landmark restaurants. He packages and freezes individual portions, which are combined with brown rice upon serving. The recipe is so tasty that visitors to Perrier's elegant Chestnut Hill home have been known to request a late-night snack of "Isabelle's food." "Our massage therapist is most definitely hooked," laughs Andrea Perrier, Georges's wife.

Isabelle was a gift to Georges, who never had a dog, from his brother and sister-in-law during a rough period in the chef's life when he was newly single. "They told me I needed company, and they gave me a dog!" he laughs. Isabelle, according to her owner, is perfect. "She's not too big, but she demands a lot of affection," Georges notes. "And she understands both English and French!" And even though Isabelle has been known to ignore commands in both languages, she remains the apple of this discerning chef's eye. "She has never eaten dog food, ever," he notes, "and when I take her for a walk, I never need a leash."

Originally from Lyon, France, Georges began his culinary career at the age of fourteen, training with some of France's legendary chefs, including Michel Lorrain, Jacques Picard, and Guy Thivard. He arrived in Philadelphia in 1967 at the age of twenty-three to take up the post of head chef for Peter von Starck's La Panetière. Three years later, he opened his signature restaurant, Le Bec-Fin (a French idiom for "the good taste"), which *Esquire* called the best French restaurant in America, and which a 1994 *Conde Nast* readers' poll ranked as the best restaurant in the country. Le Bec-Fin earned five stars—the highest culinary honor—twenty-six times from the annual *Mobil Travel Guide* (now the *Forbes Travel Guide*), and Perrier was the only chef in the country to lose the award and win it back (two years later).

The restaurant continues to receive top honors from such publications as *Gourmet, Food & Wine, Esquire,* and *Wine Spectator,* even as its owner announced

in July 2009 that he was contemplating its closure. "It's different now," said Georges at the time. "People don't want to sit for three hours. Not even me. I have owned this for [over] forty years. I've had a lot of good times and maybe I realize that Philadelphia is ready for something else." On January 1, 2011, however, champagne corks popped to celebrate the New Year as well as the fact that Perrier had changed his mind. "I have received an outpouring of letters from all over the world, begging me not to close," Georges explains, disclosing that he has plans to renovate the downstairs Le Bar Lyonnais as well as the mezzanine dining room.

The renowned chef also plans to open a bakery (The Art of Bread) in suburban

Narberth sometime in 2011 and is said to be developing a catering venture as well as a retail line of sorbets. Georges is still driven, but is perhaps *un peu* less concerned about ratings and more comfortable in his own skin. "I don't want to be judged again," he admits. He says that he is placing a premium on something that was missing during all those dog-eat-dog years: "I want to have fun."

Fun is taking Isabelle for long walks, entertaining family and friends, and, above all, keeping himself in the culinary world. "I plan to be the best for at least thirty more years," he says with a smile.

Isabelle's "TouTou" Food

Chef Georges says, "Even though Isabelle is bilingual, TouTou is French for 'doggy.' I make this recipe about once a month in my restaurant kitchen and freeze it in individual portions. You can make it in smaller batches by cutting the ingredients in half. Isabelle eats this every day, and sometimes so do human visitors to our home. It is that good!"

Dr. Khuly's note: *"Wow! One of the original celebrity chefs! While garlic and other alliums (including onions, chives, scallions, and shallots) are not recommended in large quantities or for frequent feedings due to their ability to cause anemia in dogs, they are acceptable in small quantities as called for in this recipe—even more so when they are well cooked as Chef Georges's recipe specifies."*

INGREDIENTS
10 pounds chicken breast,
    boneless and skinless
5 pounds London broil
12 carrots
10 cups haricots verts (green beans)
1 Tbsp Parmesan cheese, grated
7 garlic cloves, chopped

DIRECTIONS
Grind the meat or have your butcher do so.

Blanch the vegetables by cooking them in boiling water for 1–2 minutes, depending on your dog's preference for crunchiness, and let them cool. Dice the vegetables in a medium dice.

In a hot pan, sauté the meat until it is two-thirds of the way cooked (it will still have some pink in it but will be predominantly white [chicken] or brown [beef]). Cooking time will vary depending on the size and thickness of the pan.

Add the vegetables to the pan until well blended. Continue cooking until the meat is thoroughly cooked (all of the pink is gone). Finish with the Parmesan and garlic.

Cool and then separate into daily portions and freeze. Combine one portion with 1 cup brown rice to serve. Isabelle eats about 1½ cups twice a day. Your dog's servings will depend on his size.

Keith Roberts

and Lila

Executive Chef

- Loews Santa Monica Beach Hotel

Santa Monica, California

For as long as he can remember, California native Keith Roberts loved to cook. "When I was about ten, my dad would take me to a breakfast place with an open kitchen, and I would sit at the counter and watch the cooks," he recounts. "I started cooking breakfast for my own family that same year, and my nickname was 'Chef Boy-ar-Boy!'" By the time he was twenty-one, Keith was cooking breakfast in the kitchen of the central California golf resort that his family owned while trying to figure out how he could make a living surfing and cooking. "I figured I could travel the world and surf, cooking along the way," he admits.

In 1984, he spotted a two-line ad that listed a job opening for a cook. The restaurant was Rive Gauche in Palos Verdes, and the chef was Andre Moreau. Keith got the job the day he applied. "It was an Escoffier-style kitchen, and Chef Moreau wanted someone with little experience so he didn't have to retrain the person," Keith explains. "It was a strict apprenticeship in the classic French style, and Chef was a true perfectionist. He could tell which knife I had used to cut pastries. It was amazing training."

After one year, Chef Moreau moved to the front of the house, and Keith took over the kitchen, which he ran for six years. During that time, Rive Gauche became one of the top four restaurants in Los Angeles. Keith opened Le Beaujolais in Redondo Beach for the same owners and then moved to Orlando, where he and a business partner set about recreating the Rive Gauche concept. Keith says that, at that time, French restaurants "were just beginning to burn out" in Los Angeles, and they figured that they could have some success in Orlando.

Sure enough, Parvenu (French for "attained") won the *Orlando Sentinel's* Critics' Choice Award for number-one restaurant in Orlando the year that it opened and was dubbed "One of the Best Restaurants in All of Florida" by *Central Florida Magazine* that same year. Unfortunately, the partnership didn't last, so Keith moved back to Los Angeles. He eventually landed at the famed Players, where he updated the original Hungarian recipes of owner and original chef, Mama Weiss, for appreciative patrons.

In 1995, Keith left the freestanding restaurant world, where "it was kind of like being an actor—you needed someone to discover you," for the hospitality industry, where the career ladder was a bit more defined. After turning around the banquet and restaurant facilities at the Westins in Century City and Bonaventure, the Hilton in Torrance, and the Marriott in downtown Los Angeles, Keith settled at the Loews Santa Monica Beach Hotel, where he says he is finally able to "have fun again." "People at a resort appreciate the quality of the food," he says. "They want to be there and enjoy themselves."

Along the way, Keith racked up numerous honors for his culinary prowess, having been inducted into the Los Angeles chapter of Les Toques Blanches in 1999 and serving on its board of directors in 2002. He is also a member of the Epicurean Club of Los Angeles, has cooked for the prestigious Chaîne des

Rôtisseurs gastronomic society, and was included in Chef America's "2,000 Chefs" in 1990, the inaugural year for this award.

Keith truly does enjoy himself when he is in the kitchen, especially when that kitchen includes his dog, Lila, who is part German Shepherd and part Akita. It turns out that Lila, who was a puppy when Keith and his wife rescued her from a pound, is a well-behaved companion. "She had a respiratory infection when she was a puppy and couldn't run much, so she turned out to be very mellow, which is a good thing, because the boy for whom she was bought, our son, never

took on all the duties we expected him to," Keith explains wryly. That same respiratory infection is the reason she also doesn't bark very much. "She is a great house dog—quiet, polite, and not in need of constant attention or affection yet always ready with a smile. She makes me laugh every day," Keith admits.

Lila suits Keith and his family's lifestyle perfectly. "She's great with our son, she loves our cat, and she is very content to be top dog in a one-dog house! She also has one ear that stands up, which makes her very endearing."

Lila and Keith play a game when he gives her treats. "She refuses to eat it until I try to take it from her," he explains. "When I do, she steals it back and barks, wagging her tail. Then she will chow down." Lila performs the same antics with her dinner. "She won't eat until I come close, at which point she barks, all the while watching and wagging to make sure I am still playing!" he laughs. "Ultimately, of course, she gobbles up her food, especially if I am serving her special chow."

Lila Chow

Chef Keith says, "My special recipe for Lila is based on memories of my youth. When my mom would give chicken gizzards to our normally quiet cat, the cat would emit a primal growl and aggressively protect her 'feast.' This always made me think that this was the ultimate in eating pleasure. I tried to recreate the same experience for Lila, which is why I have included the beef tendons. Beef tendons can be found in Asian markets, and they provide a significant chew factor along with the bone marrow for the flavor 'reward.' Chicken livers, rice, and veggies round out the nutritional aspect, making it plate-lickin' good!"
He goes on to advise, "Be forewarned, however, that the beef tendons should cook for at least twelve hours. Allow yourself a full day—or two—to make this recipe. You can cook and cool the tendon, wrap it in plastic, and store it in the refrigerator overnight to make the recipe the next day. You can also cook up a bunch of large tendons and store them in the freezer until you are ready to use them, at which point you would thaw one before making the recipe."

INGREDIENTS
1 large beef tendon
½ cup beef marrow, diced small
1 cup chicken livers, chopped fine
2½ Tbsp uncooked brown rice
¼ cup raw carrots, diced small
¼ cup raw green beans, diced
1 Tbsp olive oil
 Water

DIRECTIONS
Simmer the beef tendon in enough water to cover (at least 6 cups) until tender—12 hours or longer. You can use a slow cooker on medium heat. Check periodically to see that there is still water in the pot; add more if needed.

Dice the cooked beef tendon. It should yield about ¾ cup of diced pieces.

Add the rice to ¾ cup water. Bring to a boil, then cover and reduce the heat. Simmer until the liquid is absorbed, then remove from heat.

Add the diced carrots to 1 cup of boiling water; cook for 6 minutes. Remove from heat and discard the water.

Add the diced green beans to 1 cup boiling water; cook for 1 minute. Remove from heat and discard the water.

Place the olive oil and beef marrow in a large frying pan over medium-low heat. Slowly heat until the marrow softens and starts to melt.

Turn up the heat and add the vegetables and beef tendon, stirring until evenly heated. Add the chicken livers while keeping the mixture moving; stir until cooked halfway. Add the brown rice. Heat the mixture to 165 degrees.

Cool the mixture before serving to your "guest"— and stand back!

This recipe can be stored in the refrigerator in a covered container for no more than two days or can be frozen for up to two months. Thaw before serving.

Harry Schwartz

and Blitz

**Culinary and
Creative Director**

- Heritage Trail
  Winery & Cafe

Lisbon,
Connecticut

An Iowa native with an undergraduate degree in economics and graduate studies in accounting, Chef Harry began his career about as far away from the kitchen as one can get—as president and CEO of a scrap-metal recycling company in Tulsa, Oklahoma, that he and his brother acquired in 1985. The company became one of the biggest scrap-metal processors in the region—so big, in fact, that they sold the business in 1991, and Harry, who was then thirty-four, and his wife, Laurie, retired to Jupiter Island, Florida, with their daughter. "This was before Jupiter became Jupiter," he laughs. "Celine Dion's pool is where our house once was."

A self-professed workaholic, Harry (and Laurie) had also founded Back Bay Gourmet, a trendy Tulsa restaurant, while he was building the scrap-metal business. The place was so popular that the couple sold it after six months upon receiving an unsolicited offer that they could not refuse. They went on to create the restaurant in Tulsa's Philbrook Museum of Art during the museum's expansion and began to compile a lot of wonderful recipes.

One of Harry's first projects in his "retirement" was to write two cookbooks: *Easygoing Entertaining* and *Harry's Wild About You Cookbook*. "The premise of both books became my mantra—how anyone could cook like a gourmet chef without any formal training," he says. "All it takes to be a great cook are great ingredients."

The affable and energetic Harry became a local celebrity. It wasn't long before he landed an appearance on NBC's *Today Show* to demonstrate some recipes. After his first appearance in May 1995, he became a regular. So began a love affair between Harry and the camera that continues to this day.

His stint on the *Today Show* led to an offer from PBS to create a series, *Chef Harry and Friends*, which ran for six years and two cookbooks. Harry and Laurie relocated to Malibu, California, where Harry ultimately became the food guru for the CBS affiliate in Los Angeles, wrote a syndicated column for Copley News Service, developed a radio show, and became a creative consultant and spokesperson for several corporations.

"At heart, I really am a PBS chef," he explains. "I don't yell, scream, or compete. To me, it's all about the food and sharing it with others." To date, Chef Harry has done over 3,000 segments and shows for various networks.

In 2007, Chef Harry hit the road on a national tour, "Fitness from the Start," based on his book *Fit Foundation: A Guide to Help Achieve Good Health for America's Overweight Youth*, written in conjunction with the University of Miami and PBS in 2006. Overweight in his youth, Chef Harry, who lost 100 pounds—twice—was teased as a child and knows firsthand about the low self-esteem associated with childhood obesity. He and Laurie traveled the country in a custom-built 41-foot bus outfitted with a complete kitchen and sponsored by the National Watermelon Promotion Board and Ziploc. Ironically, while on tour, Harry suffered a massive heart attack. The prescription for recovery came as no surprise: slow down.

Enter Connecticut's Heritage Trail Vineyards, which the couple purchased in 2008 and renovated, adding a restaurant and event space. "I'm trying to slow down," Harry admits, even as opportunities continue to beckon. He has developed a loyal and diverse clientele (many drive two hours from New York City for his amazing low-fat gelato), and he takes great pleasure in serving good food in a tranquil setting.

His current dog, Blitz, a Miniature Pinscher/Viszla mix, adds to his serenity (even though the dog's name is derived from "what he did to the house as a puppy"). Harry, who was never allowed to have a dog as a child, is a fervent animal lover, and he and Laurie have had many dogs, including Great Danes that they adopted from a rescue while they were living in California. "We became friends with Burt Ward, who played Robin in the *Batman* television series, and he and his wife operate a Great Dane rescue," Harry recalls. "We already had a Boston Terrier, but Laurie wanted a big dog for security. We adopted our 240-pound Great Dane, Raffiki, from the Wards' rescue, and Laurie had a torrid love affair with him!" As owners of giant breeds know, bigger dogs unfortunately live shorter lives. Heartbroken after the loss of Raffiki, the Schwartzes adopted Dauphney, another Great Dane with whom Harry found true love. "I used to make up a story that I was in love with a Danish stewardess," he jokes.

Unfortunately, Great Danes and Harry's tour buses did not mix. So after Dauphney passed, the couple went back to Boston Terriers and got Wally. "He was the most vulnerable, emotional, loving dog I had ever met," sighs Harry. It was, in fact, Wally's death ("I couldn't stop sobbing for a month," he admits) that led them to Blitz. "We were returning home from a tour, and I couldn't go into the house without a dog," Harry recalls. "My daughter ran to get the local paper, and there was one ad—for a shorthaired male pup. He was it! We met the woman an hour later and went home with an eight-week-old red mouse who we named Blitz!"

The first thing Harry did was tell Blitz the story of Wally, whose ashes he keeps in a black urn by his bed. "[Blitz] understood everything and knew that his job was to help my heart heal," Harry says. And he has. "Blitz is brilliant, beautiful, funny, soulful, and loving, and he spoons me in bed," Harry gushes. "We share a cappuccino every morning, although he just gets the foamed skim milk!"

Blitz's Pork Loin and Truffles

Chef Harry says, "Blitz has a very sensitive colon, and this recipe is based on pretty much all he can eat. It makes one serving for a dog of approximately 20 pounds."
Dr. Khuly's note: *"Beautiful presentation!"*

INGREDIENTS

Quick-cook oats, enough to make ¼ cup cooked oatmeal
3 pork loin medallions, 2 ounces each
1 tsp canola oil
6 baby carrots
2 cups low- or no-salt vegetable broth

DIRECTIONS

Cook the oats with boiling water only. Allow to cool.

Brush the pork medallions with the canola oil. Grill the pork over medium-high heat until medium-well done. Remove the pork from the grill and cool.

Poach the baby carrots in the vegetable broth until tender.
Drain and cool the carrots and reserve a small amount
of the broth. Puree the carrots with just enough of the broth
to make a saucelike texture.

With a sharp knife, cut the pork into small bits. Roll ¼ cup of oatmeal into small trufflelike balls. Spread the carrot puree artfully on a white dinner plate. Arrange the pork in a mound in the center of the puree. Dot the plate with oatmeal truffles around the mound of pork on the puree.

Serve to your begging pooch and watch it disappear!

Amaryll Schwertner

and Boulette

Chef/Owner

- Boulette's Larder

San Francisco, California

The Culinary Canine

Amaryll Schwertner was born in Budapest, Hungary, where Pulis (or Hungarian Sheepdogs) were part of her childhood. "We Hungarians have a long-established relationship with dogs as herders and hunters—working dogs," the accomplished chef says. "Pulis are iconoclasts—independent, intuitive, and clever." She might well be describing herself. A world-renowned chef, Amaryll has garnered a reputation for being able to express all of the dimensions of her personality through her culinary prowess. "I have always been interested in ingredients from all over the world, and it became my passion to understand and translate the soul of thoughtfully prepared food, no matter where it comes from," she notes.

Although she had studied neuroscience at the university level, when she immigrated to the United States with her family in 1956, Amaryll decided to pursue the culinary arts, influenced in part by her maternal grandmother's cooking. Since the early 1980s, Amaryll has been cooking in San Francisco, most recently at her spectacular location in the restored Ferry Building Marketplace. She opened Boulette's Larder with her partner, Lori Regis, in 2003. The restaurant, named after their Puli, serves breakfast and lunch every day and is available after-hours for private parties ranging in size from two to twenty-four. While she won't drop names, Amaryll confirms that her restaurant is the preferred choice of those who "don't want to be seen" and mentions that she has served many "famous people."

In fact, Amaryll holds her own when it comes to celebrity, having been nominated by the legendary Alice Waters for inclusion in *Coco: 10 World-Leading Masters Choose 100 Contemporary Chefs*. This is an extreme honor, as the top chefs in the world determined the selections. Boulette's Larder has also received rave reviews in such publications as the *Wall Street Journal*, the *San Francisco Examiner*, *Esquire*, the *New York Times*, and *Metropolitan Home*.

Amaryll has cooked for Boulette since she was a pup, developing the recipe for canine boulettes. As she explains, "The French word *boulette*...literally translates to 'little ball.' The culinary references are [to] little meatballs [made of lamb], as in Moroccan cuisine, or little balls of fresh French goat cheese." Canine boulettes began as a clever way to make use of the restaurant's leftover chicken stock, made every day from whole organic chickens, and the remains of the nine-grain-and-seed cereal prepared every morning. Boulettes for human patrons soon followed, and both items have become staples of the "larder" portion of the restaurant, a take-out market with prepared foods and high-quality pantry items. "We make many different kinds of boulettes," Amaryll notes. "For people, some are meat, some are cheese, and some are seafood. The ones for dogs [are sold as] organic dog food."

Just like all of the dishes in her restaurant, the boulettes for pets are prepared from fresh, organic ingredients. Amaryll has long been an advocate of sourcing

sustainable food, and she has nurtured the efforts of local farmers as well as the development of urban farmers' markets. Selling dog food along with "people food" is just a natural extension of this philosophy. "Why shouldn't you buy food for your dog where you buy food for yourself?" she laughs.

As for Boulette, she is a walking endorsement for the food that bears her name, and she treats each and every meal with quiet reverence. "She has a habit of contemplating her food," Amaryll explains. "She lies down 3 to 4 feet from her bowl and faces it—then, five minutes later, she approaches it and eats slowly, unlike most other dogs we've known."

One of the most distinctive qualities of the Puli breed is its coat, which resembles human dreadlocks. According to Amaryll, the "ribbons" of hair, which have a protective function in the field, form when the dogs are around six months old; because it is hair, not fur, the dogs do not shed. "There is never any brushing," Amaryll laughs. "The hair stays furled when it is wet, and it takes a very long time to dry. It is all very familiar to me since these are the dogs I remember from my youth."

Boulette's Larder Pet Boulettes

Chef Amaryll says, "Many dog and cat owners purchase our pet boulettes. A testament to their quality is the comment of a customer's husband who, left to his own resources, found an unmarked package of pet boulettes in the freezer and enthusiastically made dinner. He told his wife upon her return that the dinner was delicious, with the minor addition of some salt!"

INGREDIENTS
4 organic carrots
2 whole organic chicken breasts
Enough dried multigrain cereal (such as
    oats, millet, or barley) to make 2 cups
    hot porridge
½ Tbsp ground flax
½ Tbsp ground sesame seeds
½ Tbsp brewer's yeast
Parsley (optional)
Blueberries (optional)

DIRECTIONS
Poach the carrots and the two chicken breasts on the bone without salt in 4 cups of water until they are moist and fully cooked. Do not reduce them to a pasty consistency—leave some nice texture. Reserve the chicken broth.

Cool the chicken breasts and carrots and then grind them in a food processor or dice by hand to the consistency preferred by your pet. For larger dogs, a bigger dice that gives a chunkier texture is good. Smaller dogs and/or cats may prefer smaller pieces and a smoother texture.

Prepare 2 cups of multigrain porridge in 4 cups of the broth left over from poaching the chicken breasts and carrots. Let the porridge sit to cool.

Combine the chicken breast and carrots with the cooked grain cereal, ground flax, ground sesame seeds, and brewer's yeast. Parsley and/or fresh blueberries may be added if available. Cool the mixture and then form into 3-ounce patties (boulettes). The boulettes keep in the refrigerator for two days or can be frozen for future use.

• For small dogs, serve one boulette mixed with organic kibble once daily.
• For medium dogs, serve two boulettes mixed with organic kibble once daily.
• For large dogs, serve two boulettes mixed with organic kibble twice daily.
• For cats, serve one-half to one boulette mixed with organic cat food once daily.

Nicholas Shipp

and Gnocchi

Executive Chef

- Upper West

Santa Monica,
California

The Culinary Canine

Nicholas Shipp began his culinary career at the age of fifteen, washing dishes in a local restaurant in Fort Worth, Texas. When the cook didn't show up one night, he filled in—permanently. While he loved the restaurant business, his primary passion was playing the drums. In the end, though, Nicholas decided to attend the Culinary Institute of Dallas, foregoing a potential career in the music business. He has never regretted the choice.

After graduating, Nick moved to Los Angeles, where he had the opportunity to work for the Wolfgang Puck franchise. He spent two years crafting his skills before becoming executive chef at Pete's Café in downtown Los Angeles, where he developed his palate for modern American/global cuisine.

As executive chef at Upper West, Nick works in an open kitchen and turns out innovative takes on American cuisine. He calls it "sexy comfort food," combining "crazy mixtures of ingredients and cultures" that he feels reflect the Los Angeles vibe. Not one to take himself too seriously ("At the end of the day, it's just food," he smiles), Nick has made a name for himself with his sophisticated yet comfortable American food with a contemporary twist.

Perhaps his affinity for disparity is why Nick, a big guy, fell hard and fast for his Yorkshire Terrier, Gnocchi. "I wasn't planning on getting a dog, but if I did, I was thinking along the lines of a Bulldog," he admits. "But when my wife and I saw Gnocchi, we couldn't imagine not sharing our lives with him." All of 3 pounds, Gnocchi was six months old before he almost filled the palm of Nick's hand. "When we first got him, he looked like a furball waddling down the hall," Nick laughs. Believe it or not, that little furball came with a stubborn streak ("Like his papa," Nick laughs), although he is always loving and a source of continual amusement.

Named for one of Nick's favorite foods, Gnocchi gets along beautifully with the Shipps' baby daughter. "The baby, who was [born] two months early, was two times the size of the puppy," he says. "Gnocchi is very protective of my daughter—almost like an older brother. He is truly amazing, and I think he is perfect for our family. In fact, he is family."

Yorkie Lamb Stew with Mint Cilantro Crunch

Chef Nick says, "This is an easy rice and lamb-based stew for the home cook. Gnocchi swears by it! You will need a 6-quart slow cooker and a 12-inch frying pan to make this dish."

INGREDIENTS

For the stew:
1 Tbsp vegetable oil
1 pound ground lamb
5 cups water
3 medium potatoes, diced small (for extra flavor, use Yukon Gold)
2 broccoli stalks, diced small
3 medium raw carrots, diced small
2 cups uncooked brown rice
1 Tbsp cracked pepper

For the crunch:
2 small mint-flavored dog biscuits
2 Tbsp chopped cilantro

DIRECTIONS

Heat the oil in a frying pan. Brown the lamb and the potatoes in the same pan over medium heat. Remove from heat.

Boil the water in a separate pot and add it to the slow cooker.

Add the broccoli and carrots to the slow cooker. Strain off any excess grease from the lamb and potatoes, then add the lamb/potato mix and the uncooked rice to the slow cooker. If needed, add more water to the slow cooker so that all of the ingredients are covered with water.

Add the cracked pepper and cover the slow cooker. Cook on low heat until the lamb is well cooked—at least 3 to 4 hours, depending on your slow cooker's thermostat. Let the stew cool.

For the crunch, simply crush the two dog biscuits and mix the pieces with the chopped cilantro.

To serve, put the stew in your best friend's bowl and top with the crunch.

Jay Silva

and Brock

Executive Chef

- Bambara, a Kimpton Restaurant

Cambridge, Massachusetts

Massachusetts native Jay Silva learned to cook the same way that every one of the ten children in his family did: by pitching in at family mealtime. "My mother was a great cook, and dinner was an important part of our upbringing," he explains. As one of the youngest, he remembers his responsibilities being more "busywork" than actual technique, but he developed a love for food and cooking that he missed after a stint in the Air Force following high school. "I had worked summers as a dishwasher and for one of my brothers who had a sandwich shop on the Cape," he remembers. "Culinary school seemed like a logical step."

A graduate of Newbury College's culinary program, Jay honed his skills in some of Boston's finest kitchens, including those of the Boston Harbor Hotel, the Ritz-Carlton Boston, Pigalle, Sage, and Pho Republique. Jay calls his cuisine at Bambara "seasonal, creative American." While he is trained in French, Italian, and Asian techniques, he tries to stay away from overlapping too many flavors, preferring to let the food "speak for itself." "It really makes sense for my style of

cooking to rely heavily on local, seasonal ingredients," he continues. Jay's menu at Bambara largely reflects his Massachusetts's native-son status and includes such favorites as lobster sliders, "lobster chowdah," and rock shrimp risotto.

Having grown up with German Shepherds, Jay longed for the day when his schedule would permit him to have a dog of his own. After purchasing a house with his girlfriend, who had grown up with Labrador Retrievers, the timing seemed right, but the couple remained undecided about the breed until they happened upon the Viszla while watching the Westminster Kennel Club Dog Show on television in 2010. "I really wanted a shorthaired dog, so when we spotted the Viszla, we started to do some research," he says. "It turned out to be the perfect breed for us."

Brock came from a family in upstate New York. "We met both [of Brock's] parents, who were actual hunting dogs, and they had only one litter," Jay says. In fact, Brock has proved to be such a poster child for the breed that one of the servers at Bambara, who once dog-sat Brock, got a Viszla of his own! "They're active but not hyper, very trainable, and supersmart," Jay notes. "[Brock's] a really good dog, and I'm really proud of him. He's definitely a member of the family."

Brock's Lamb Tartare

*Chef Jay says, "I like to use sushi rice, as it has a nice, creamy quality.
Either way, your dog should gobble this up!"*

INGREDIENTS
4 ounces raw lamb scraps
1 egg
1 carrot
¼ cup rice, cooked

DIRECTIONS
Finely dice the lamb scraps. Set aside.

Put the entire egg, including the shell, into a food
processor or blender and blend well.

Shred the carrot in a food processor or with a grater.

Mix all of the ingredients together with the rice
in a mixing bowl.

Serve in a dog bowl, but watch your fingers!

Guillermo Tellez

and Milee

Executive Chef

- Square 1682,
  a Kimpton
  Restaurant

Philadelphia,
Pennsylvania

The Culinary Canine

When Guillermo Tellez was thirteen, he left his native Mexico for the United States. He ended up in Chicago, where a friend asked him to help wash dishes at an International House of Pancakes. It was there he realized that his future involved a kitchen. "I loved the environment, the feeling of camaraderie among the workers. It felt right," the veteran executive chef says. He took classes during the day and worked in restaurants at night until he racked up degrees from Kendall College's School for the Culinary Arts in Chicago and Madeleine Kamman's School for American Chefs at Beringer Vineyards in Napa Valley. He was passionate about food, cooking, and bettering himself.

This passion was recognized by none other than Charlie Trotter, the well-known Chicago chef and restaurateur. In 1989, Guillermo began a worldly career that became synonymous not only with Trotter but also with excellence. He traveled the globe to learn the sophisticated cuisines of other countries, developing and executing recipes that reflected this knowledge. Guillermo ultimately landed in Las Vegas, where he became chef de cuisine at Charlie Trotter's restaurant at the MGM Grand. Shortly thereafter, he was named the first winner of the James Beard Foundation's Felipe Rojas-Lombardi Award of Achievement for Hispanic Chefs.

More accolades followed and opportunities ensued, one of which was to open "C," a Charlie Trotter restaurant, in a Los Cabos, Mexico, resort. It was here that Guillermo rubbed elbows with Barbra Streisand and other celebrities who frequented the pet-friendly establishment with their dogs. In fact, Guillermo developed a dog-friendly "tasting menu" for Ms. Streisand's pooches. Shortly after it opened, "C" was listed as a "Best of the Best" by the *Robb Report*.

In 2005, Guillermo moved to New York to open another restaurant for Charlie Trotter. The economy put that plan on hold, so he took a job with the hospitality giant Sodexo, a provider of food and facilities management services across the United States. In his consultant role, Guillermo helped redesign corporate dining facilities for both HBO and Merrill Lynch. In 2007, Stephen Starr, the Philadelphia restaurateur, hired him to develop menus and concepts for several new restaurants.

The Culinary Canine

Since 2010, Guillermo has been back in his beloved kitchen as executive chef at Square 1682 in Philadelphia. The multitalented chef may be at his best when he is busy combining the flavors of the world into new versions of classic dishes, always emphasizing freshness and ecologically sound culinary practices.

The most recent addition to the Tellez family (Guillermo and his wife, pastry chef Leslie Swager, have two daughters) is Milee, a Maltese/Yorkshire Terrier mix. Although they have had big dogs in the past, everyone loves the fact that Milee is so portable. "You can put her in your pocket and take her anywhere," Guillermo laughs. "And we do." Milee has even been camping! The tiny pooch is not overwhelmed by much, and she seems to have a sense of her limits. "If a dog in the park is too big or too rough, she just sits down until he leaves her alone," Guillermo explains. "We are all in love with her."

Milee's Mexican Treats

Chef Guillermo says, "Maybe it is the chorizo in these treats that gives Milee her energy, or maybe she is just one happy puppy! Either way, the Spanish sausage gives these snacks a nice kick."

INGREDIENTS

2 ounces hard Spanish chorizo
2⅓ cups flour (all-purpose or whole-wheat)
¼ cup olive oil
¼ cup applesauce
½ cup grated cheese (such as Parmesan)
1 large egg
1 tsp garlic powder
¼ cup nonfat powdered milk

DIRECTIONS

Mince the chorizo, then sauté it in a hot frying pan until crispy—about 4 minutes. Transfer it to paper towels to remove the excess fat. Blot and cool.

When the chorizo is cool, combine all of the ingredients in a large bowl and mix well to create a dough.

Roll the dough out to about 9 inches by 13 inches, then pat the dough onto a lightly greased 9- by 13-inch cookie sheet, bringing it to the edges. Use a sharp knife or a pizza cutter to score the dough (do not cut all the way through) into pieces of the desired size. (If you are going to use the cookies as training treats, score the dough into small pieces.) Sprinkle a little more cheese onto the dough for extra flavor.

Bake in a 350-degree oven for about 15 minutes or until golden brown. Turn off the oven and let the treats cool for a few hours. The longer you leave them, the more they will harden.

Break the treats apart and store them either tightly covered or in the freezer.

Dana Tommasino and Margie Conard

and Chickpea

**Chef/Co-owner
and Co-owner**

- Woodward's Garden

San Francisco,
California

The Culinary Canine

In 1985, when Dana Tommasino moved to San Francisco from Santa Monica to attend California Culinary Academy, her landlord warned her not to bring any cockroaches into the building. "Let's just say, back then it was hardly 'hip' to be a chef," she laughs. What a difference in the perception today! Chef Tommasino is among the early adopters of the farm-to-table movement. She continues to turn out seasonally inspired meals in a gem of a restaurant, Woodward's Garden, in the artsy Mission District. The restaurant, which she has co-owned since 1992 with culinary-school classmate Margie Conard, is located under the freeway, on the site of the original Woodward's Gardens amusement park. (The park operated from 1866 to 1891 and featured balloon rides, a zoo, a roller-skating rink, and other attractions.) Margie runs the front of the house, and Dana heads the kitchen, but they create the menus—which change nightly—together.

Dana earned a master's degree in literature from Mills College; Margie has a BA in American studies from the University of California, Santa Cruz, and the pair brings an academic component to the restaurant. One reviewer has described the space, which is predominantly occupied by an exposed kitchen, as suggestive of "the romantic overtones of an E. L. Doctorow novel." Poetry dinners and readings are popular at Woodward's Garden, and the friendly neighborhood spot has been likened to favorite haunts in Paris, complete with the "salon" atmosphere.

All of the food is locally sourced and lovingly prepared, reflecting Dana's early career as a strictly vegetarian chef at Greens Restaurant as well as Margie's training at Postrio, part of the Wolfgang Puck empire. The two owners' hands-on approach ensures that Woodward's Garden is both distinctive and comfortable, a place where the food is artfully created, beautifully executed, and served in a manner that is both personal and professional.

Dana and Margie got Chickpea, their Norwich Terrier, because they fell in love with a friend's dog, Coco (pictured), whom they often dog-sat. "We were told that Coco was a Norwich Terrier, but...they really don't look the same," Dana laughs. No matter. The two dogs are best friends and share the same fun-loving temperament and spirit. "Norwiches are spirited, loyal, curious, and adaptable. A friend once called Chickpea a 'fairy-tale hedgehog.' Who wouldn't want all that?" Dana asks.

Chickpea was a gift to their daughter Claire for her sixth birthday, but as every parent knows, taking care of a pet is a family affair. "We're a small family in a small home," Dana elaborates. "She's a small dog with a big personality—a bit like having a cartoon character in our lives. In fact, she's scared of Chihuahuas but loves Great Danes! She's always on point, doing her job, patrolling the door,

and making sure that everything is in order. But when she does finally relax, it's total charm. In fact, she's the only dog we've known who will sleep on the pillow just above your head, and she wakes us up every morning by licking our faces."

Her name is a culinary reference to her color, her size, and the fact that chickpeas are known for their versatility and distinctive flavor. Chickpea the canine is devoted to her family and gives them all "high-fives" when they come home. "She snorts, squeals, and runs her little paws when she dreams," Dana sighs. "Every moment is the best with her."

Goat Shanks with Fennel, Coriander, and Honey

Chef Dana says, "Goat meat, which is attaining some vogue now, is especially lean—the new 'white meat.' If you can't find it, substitute lamb shanks. And do try to find sustainably farmed meat, which is just better on many levels. While this is a fairly mild braise, it is also flavor-packed enough for both you and your pooch. I mean, as long as you're bothering to make a proper braise, why not? Or you could freeze the leftovers to be shared—or not."

INGREDIENTS

6 meaty goat or lamb shanks,
   preferably grass fed
Sea salt
Freshly ground pepper
4 Tbsp olive oil
2 medium bulbs fennel, cut in half
   lengthwise, then into ¼-inch slices
   lengthwise
1 large pinch of saffron threads,
   lightly finger-crushed
¾ cup fresh tomatoes, peeled and chopped,
   or good boxed/canned chopped tomatoes
2 Tbsp honey
1 cinnamon stick
4 cups chicken stock or water
½ bunch fresh coriander (cilantro),
   stem and all, tied with butcher string

DIRECTIONS

Preheat oven to 375 degrees. Salt and pepper the goat shanks. On top of the stove, heat a large, deep Dutch oven that can hold all of the meat. Add 2 tablespoons of the olive oil and brown the meat over medium-high heat, turning every few minutes to brown all sides. Remove the shanks from the dish and set aside. Add the last 2 tablespoons of oil to the Dutch oven. Add the fennel and cook for about 5 minutes. Add the saffron and cook for another 5 minutes. Add the tomatoes, honey, and cinnamon and cook for a few more minutes. Add the stock and bring to a simmer.

Tuck the shanks back into the pot along with the tied cilantro. Cover and braise in the oven until tender, about 3 hours. Check every so often; add more liquid if necessary. Cooking is finished when the meat is buttery and falling off the bone. Taste; season with salt and pepper as necessary.

Cool significantly, then carefully remove the meat from one of the shanks for your pooch. Mix with a bit of the pan sauce and serve. (You can have yours whole, on a plate.)

Eileen Watkin

and Kasey

Executive Chef

- ## The Inn at Penn

Philadelphia,
Pennsylvania

The Culinary Canine

When you live in the city, you have to be creative in keeping an energetic dog busy—which is where leaping over park benches comes in. Eileen Watkin, executive chef at the Hilton Inn at Penn in Philadelphia, taught her Lab/Pit Bull mix, Kasey, to jump first through hula hoops and then over park benches. "She likes to jump anyway, so I thought it would be a good way for her to burn off some steam," the Philadelphia native smiles.

The plan worked beautifully. Kasey is perfectly content to clear benches, fetch her Frisbee, and sometimes just roll in the grass, as long as Eileen doles out praise and treats. The same strategy works for Eileen in the kitchen, where she

marshals her kitchen staff with a firm hand and lots of patience. "The approach is similar," she admits. "Positive reinforcement is a powerful tool."

Eileen attributes her love of all things culinary to her mother, who loved to experiment with diverse and interesting cuisines. Eileen followed her passion to the Culinary Institute of America, where she scored an internship at Commander's Palace in New Orleans. It was there, from the late chef Jamie Shannon, that Eileen learned the benefits of an organized, well-run, and consistent kitchen.

Following her graduation in 1997, she returned to Philadelphia to work under Francesco Martorella and Chris Scarduzio at Brasserie Perrier.

From there, she moved to the Ritz-Carlton Philadelphia, which opened in 2000 and for which Eileen helped create a selection of contemporary American dishes focusing on organic produce. She then became chef de cuisine at Penne, the upscale bistro on the ground floor of the Inn at Penn on the University of Pennsylvania campus.

In her current position at the Inn at Penn, the emphasis is on local and seasonal ingredients. Eileen describes her fare as "fresh, bright flavors that create a stimulating, appealing, balanced experience for all parts of the palate."

Eileen is delighted to remain on the Penn campus, in close proximity to her friends at Penne. It was, in fact, the front-of-the-house manager at Penne who brought Eileen and Kasey together in 2003. "[Kasey] was the last pup left from her dog's litter, and she needed a home," says Eileen simply. The two have been jumping for joy ever since.

Brown Rice Arancini with Sweet Potato and Ground Chicken

Chef Eileen says, "Arancini are a Sicilian-style finger food that literally translates to 'little oranges.' In reality, they are rice fritters (although not fried for dogs) that may be filled with a variety of meat and vegetable fillings. Kasey loves sweet potatoes and chicken, so that's what I've used in this recipe."

INGREDIENTS

1 sweet potato
1½ cups short-grain brown rice
2 Tbsp olive oil
3¾ cups low-sodium chicken broth
½ cup grated Parmesan cheese
1 whole egg
1 cup spinach, steamed and chopped fine
1 cup ground chicken, cooked

DIRECTIONS

Roast the sweet potato at 350 degrees for 40–50 minutes until tender. Scoop the flesh from the skin, then mash the flesh with a fork. Set aside.

Cook the rice risotto-style: heat the chicken broth in a saucepan to a simmer. Set aside. Heat the olive oil over medium heat in a heavy-bottomed saucepan. Add the rice and sauté for 1 minute until it becomes translucent and well coated with oil. Keeping the saucepan over medium heat, ladle in one-third of the chicken broth and stir until all of the liquid is incorporated. Add another third of the broth and, again, stir until all of it is absorbed. Repeat with the final third of chicken broth.

Stir half of the Parmesan into the cooked rice. Allow the rice to cool slightly—about 5 minutes.

Whisk the egg in a bowl and temper in some hot rice. Incorporate the rest of the rice. Work quickly so as not to scramble the egg.

Place one-quarter of the egg/rice mixture into a food processor and puree it until smooth. Stir the pureed mixture back into the rest of the rice, then set aside and allow the rice to cool to room temperature.

Combine the sweet potato, spinach, remaining Parmesan cheese, and chicken; this will be the filling. Set aside.

To fill the arancini:
Have a bowl of warm water at hand to keep your fingers clean and the rice from sticking to you. Dip your hands into the water, then take a ¼-cup-sized chunk of rice into the palm of your hand. Flatten the rice out to a disk about 2½ inches in diameter (or about the size of your palm). Place 1½ teaspoons of the chicken filling in the center and gently fold the rice around the filling. Roll into a uniform ball and set aside on a baking sheet. Repeat the process until all of the rice and filling is used up.

Serve them cold or coat them with egg, dip them in whole-wheat bread crumbs, and bake them at 350 degrees for 12 minutes on a lightly oiled baking sheet.

Offer one or two arancini to your dog as a treat. They keep in the refrigerator for about five days and can be frozen for up to two months.

Eli Zabar
and Toby and Mini

Owner

- E.A.T.
- Eli's Bread
- Eli's Vinegar Factory
- Eli's Manhattan
- T.A.S.T.E. Restaurant and Wine Bar
- W.I.N.E.

New York, New York

The Culinary Canine

You don't have to be from New York to make the connection between the Zabar name and bagels, smoked fish, and pastrami. In 1934, Eli's parents, the late Louis and Lillian, founded the original Zabar's on the corner of 80th and Broadway, and his two older brothers, Saul and Stanley, continue to run the family establishment. Youngest son Eli decided to "go east" with his visions of a different kind of experience, and his Upper East Side gourmet food stores and restaurants have become institutions of their own.

It all started with E.A.T., the gourmet deli and café at 1064 Madison Avenue that has been turning out fresh salads, overstuffed sandwiches on delicious thinly sliced bread, and flaky croissants since 1973. In 1977, Eli opened an E.A.T. "boutique" in the department store Henri Bendel, followed in 1982 by the second freestanding E.A.T. location at Madison Avenue and East 72nd Street in the Rhinelander mansion. In 1985, he sold his lease on the Rhinelander space to Ralph Lauren, closed up the boutique in Henri Bendel's, and opened E.A.T. Gifts next door to his flagship restaurant.

The bread at E.A.T. became so popular that, in 1985, Eli began a wholesale bakery operation that sold bread to local restaurants, which led to the opening in 1992 of Eli's Bread, a 15,000-square-foot bakery on East 91st Street that services more than 1,000 restaurants across the city. And what's bread without condiments? In 1993, Eli opened the Vinegar Factory, a grocery store and café (with rooftop greenhouses in which he grows his own tomatoes, salad greens, grapes, figs, and herbs) in the building that housed the last vinegar and mustard factory in New York. Eli's Manhattan, a 20,000-square-foot market modeled after the food halls prevalent in Europe, opened on Third Avenue in 1998; this was followed in 2002 by T.A.S.T.E. Restaurant & Wine Bar and W.I.N.E. shop, located right next door. He opened a summer ice cream store in Eli's Manhattan in 2005 and added a kosher bakery in 2006. In short, it is nothing less than an empire, all of which he attends to daily in his signature khaki pants, white sneakers, and button-down shirt.

Every morning, Eli can be spotted in Central Park, walking his two Soft Coated Wheaten Terriers—the dogs he swore he would never have. "My twin boys, Sasha and Oliver, began clamoring for a dog when they were about eight...and I adamantly refused," he admits. "We did make a small research project out of their interest in dogs, however, and went to visit a breeder or two. We ruled out Clumber Spaniels—very cute dogs, but more like owning a piece of furniture. And when we came home covered with dog hair after playing with some Corgis in Central Park, they were nixed by my wife. She only wears black. 'Now you know why the Queen of England wears tweeds,' she told me."

No research was involved, however, when Eli and his boys met a Soft Coated Wheaten Terrier puppy in the park. "In all honesty, and like most true love stories, this one was random and totally unexpected," he admits. "We fell, and we fell hard." The next day, Toby, a littermate of the park puppy, came home with them to stay. "The kids picked the name," says Eli. "Toby always looked so sad when he was home and so happy in the park with other dogs, so we got a second Wheaten to cheer Toby up. The kids named this one Mini. It was the era of Austin Powers ('Mini-Me'), and Mini looked small next to Toby. Toby did not cheer up. We realized he just has a sad-sack face."

The Culinary Canine

According to Eli, his dogs are "just bright enough to get what they want. Toby is very willful and Mini is sweeter and more docile, the typical second child." Though the boys intended to take care of the dogs, Eli admits that he and his wife, Devon Fredericks, "have been the walkers, brushers, feeders, doctors for all these years." In the process, he says, the couple "has spent many happy hours in Central Park, met and enjoyed the company of other dog-walkers, and, in general, had our lives enriched by these sweet, furry guys."

Bread Soup for Dogs

Eli says, "Another way to use these same ingredients is to slice the baguette into rounds and make sandwiches, using the dog food as filling. These can be served as individual treats or put into their dishes with hot chicken stock to soften. Either way, our dogs, Mini and Toby, love bread—preferably from Zabar's!" The recipe below is intended for two medium-sized dogs, but you can adjust the amounts based on how many dogs you have and how big they are.

INGREDIENTS
Half of a French baguette
2 cups hot chicken stock (homemade, please—see directions)
½ cup of your dog's favorite wet food

DIRECTIONS
Split the baguette in two directions, and then cut into ½-inch slices. You should end up with a lot of small cubes.

Divide the cubes between two dog dishes. Add ¼ cup of dog food to each dish, followed by 1 cup of hot chicken stock.

Using a fork, mash the dog food into the liquid. It should start to look like gravy, and the bread should start to soften.

Serve to two hungry pooches!

An easy way to make chicken stock: Whenever you finish a rotisserie chicken, throw the carcass in a pot with water to cover. Add whatever vegetables you have around, such as carrots, celery, and scallions, along with herbs and a bay leaf. Bring to a boil and then simmer awhile. Strain and save in the refrigerator for three or four days or in the freezer for up to three months.

Recipes:

Restaurants and Businesses: